"THE D&A³ COOKBOOK CUISINE" IS NOT JUST A COLLECTION OF RECIPES; IT'S A REFLECTION OF BONDS SHARED AND THE VALUES HELD DEAR.

WITH EACH PAGE TURNED, MAY YOU TASTE THE FLAVORS OF HERITAGE AND WARMTH OF THE FILIPINO ROOTS. LET THIS BE A CELEBRATION OF A JOURNEY, EMBRACING VEGETARIAN CUISINE WHILE HONORING THE FILIPINA-STYLED TRADITIONS THAT SHAPES US. AS WE EXPLORE THE CULINARY WORLD WITHIN THESE PAGES, MAY EVERY RECIPE BRING JOY AND INSPIRATION OF NEW ONES.

WITH LOVE & THANKSGIVING

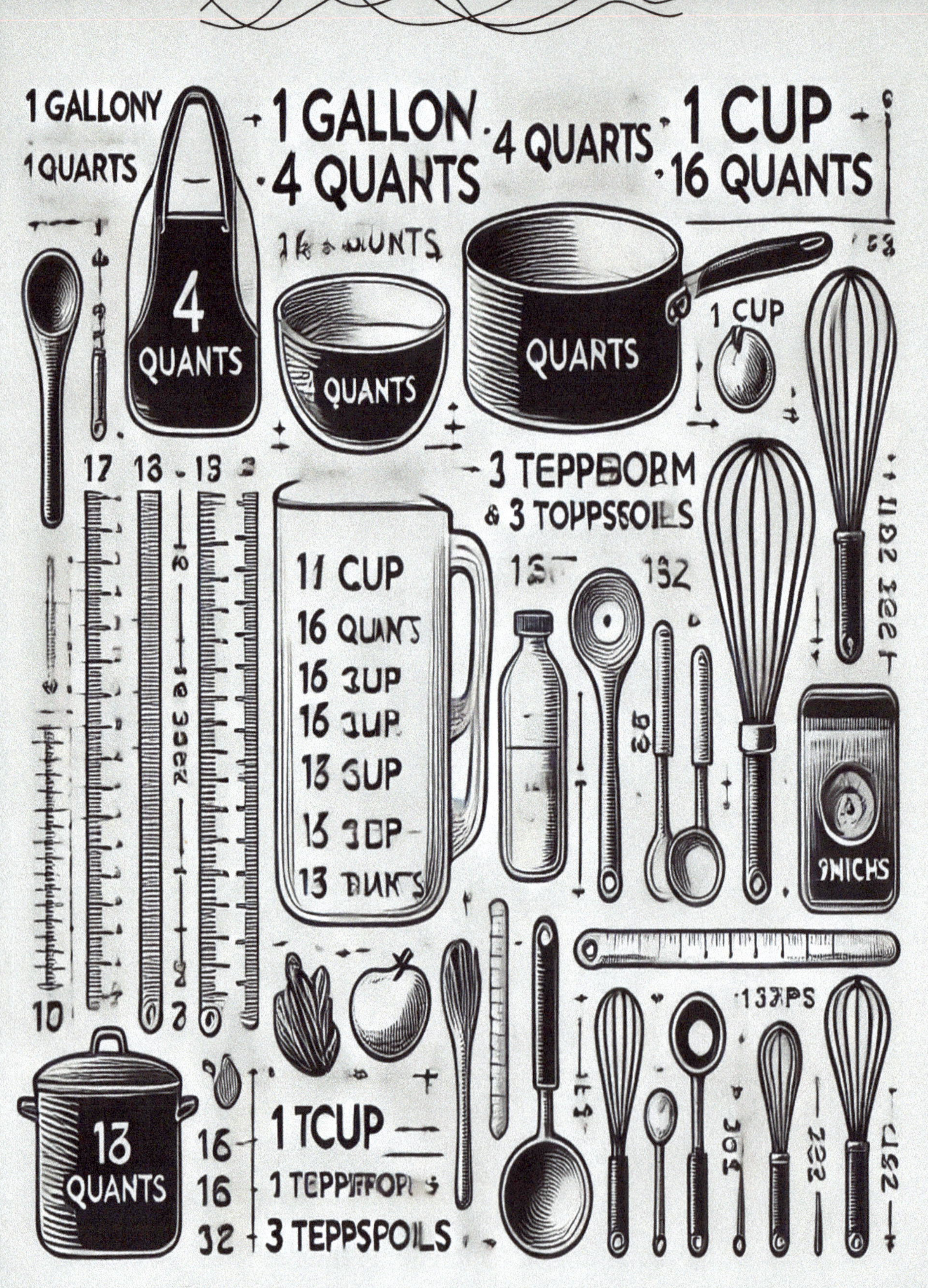

1 GALLONY
1 QUARTS
1 GALLON
4 QUANTS
4 QUARTS
1 CUP
16 QUANTS
4
QUANTS
QUANTS
QUARTS
1 CUP
3 TEPPBORM
& 3 TOPPSSOILS
11 CUP
16 QUANTS
16 3UP
16 1UP
13 SUP
15 3DP
13 BUK'S
9NICHS
13TPS
13
QUANTS
1 TCUP
1 TEPPIFOPL S
3 TEPPSPOILS

# CONTENTS

## Appetizers



## Soups & Porridge



## Main Dishes



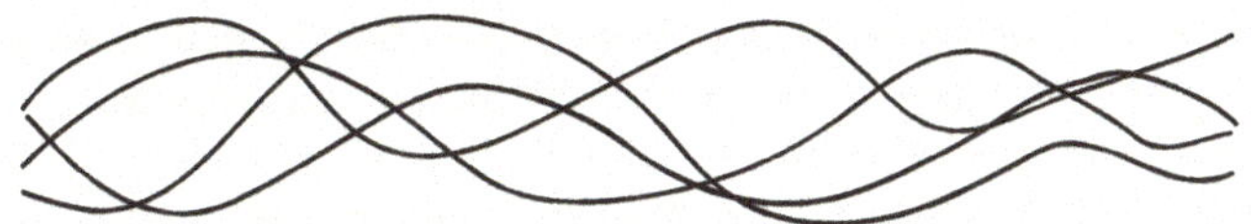

# CONTENTS

## Main Dishes



## Noodles & Rice Dishes



## Vegetarian Meat Alternatives



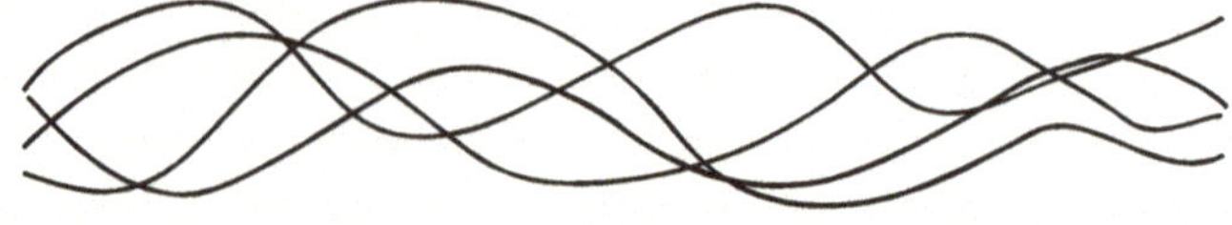

# CONTENTS

## Desserts & Sweets



## Personal Specials



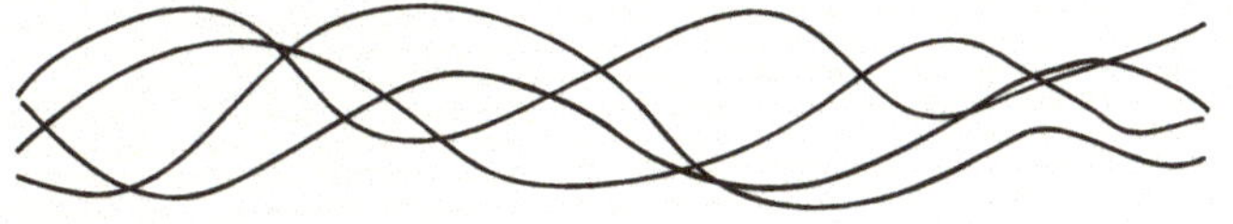

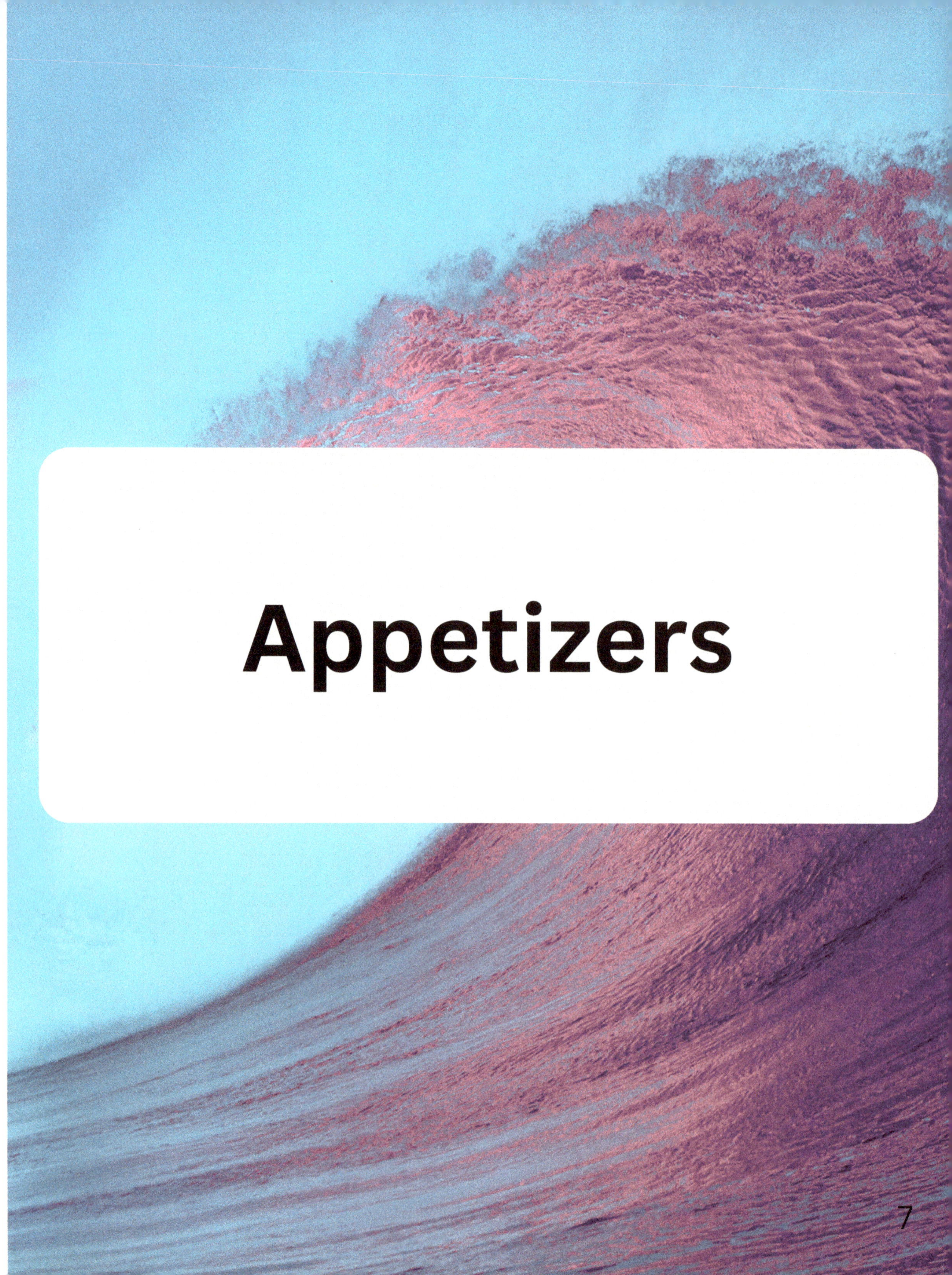

Appetizers

# Okoy

## INGREDIENTS

- 1 cup shredded sweet potatoes
- 1/2 cup bean sprouts
- 1/2 cup grated carrots
- 1/2 cup all-purpose flour
- 1/4 cup cornstarch
- 1/2 tsp baking powder
- 1/2 cup water
- 1/2 tsp salt
- 1/2 tsp ground black pepper
- Cooking oil for frying

A crispy Filipino vegetable fritter made with shredded sweet potatoes, bean sprouts, and carrots, bound in a light batter and deep-fried to golden perfection. Served with a side of spiced vinegar dipping sauce, this crunchy snack is perfect for any occasion.

- In a bowl, mix flour, cornstarch, baking powder, water, salt, and black pepper to form a light batter.
- Add shredded sweet potatoes, bean sprouts, and grated carrots. Mix well.
- Heat oil in a frying pan.
- Scoop small portions of the mixture into the hot oil and flatten slightly.
- Fry until golden brown and crispy on both sides.
- Drain excess oil and serve hot with spiced vinegar dipping sauce.

## Notes

# Kwek-Kwek

## INGREDIENTS

- 12 quail eggs, boiled and peeled
- 1/2 cup all-purpose flour
- 1/4 cup cornstarch
- 1/2 cup water
- 1 tsp annatto powder (for orange color)
- 1/2 tsp salt
- 1/2 tsp black pepper
- Cooking oil for deep frying

A popular Filipino street food featuring boiled quail eggs coated in an orange-colored batter and deep-fried until crispy. Served on a banana leaf-lined plate with spiced vinegar and sweet dipping sauce, this dish is perfect for a delicious street food experience.

- In a bowl, mix flour, cornstarch, annatto powder, salt, and pepper.
- Gradually add water while whisking to form a smooth batter.
- Coat the boiled quail eggs evenly in the batter.
- Heat oil in a pan and deep-fry the coated eggs until golden and crispy.
- Drain excess oil and serve hot with spiced vinegar or sweet dipping sauce.

Notes

# Chicharron

## INGREDIENTS

- 10-12 sheets of tofu skin or yuba
- Cooking oil for frying
- Salt or your choice of seasoning (such as barbecue seasoning or chili powder) to taste

Vegetarian chicharon made with tofu skin or yuba provides a crispy and flavorful alternative to the traditional pork version. Enjoy this vegetarian snack with your favorite dip and savor the crunchy texture!

- Soak the tofu skin or yuba in warm water for about 5 minutes to soften them.
- Once the tofu skin is soft, carefully pat it dry with paper towels to remove excess moisture.
- Cut the tofu skin into small rectangular pieces or desired shapes.
- Heat cooking oil in a deep pan or pot to a medium-high temperature for frying.
- Carefully add the tofu skin pieces to the hot oil, one at a time, and fry them until they turn golden brown and crispy. Be cautious as the oil may splatter.
- Use a slotted spoon or tongs to remove the fried tofu skin from the oil and place them on a paper towel-lined plate to drain excess oil.
- Sprinkle salt or your choice of seasoning over the fried tofu skin while they are still hot, ensuring they are evenly coated.
- Allow the vegetarian chicharon to cool slightly before serving.
- Serve the vegetarian chicharon as a snack or appetizer with a dipping sauce of your choice, such as vinegar with chopped garlic or a spicy vinegar dip.

Notes

# Lumpiang Shanghai

## INGREDIENTS

- Lumpia wrappers (spring roll wrappers)
- 2 cups cabbage, finely shredded
- 1 cup carrots, julienned or finely grated
- 1 cup bean sprouts
- 1 cup tofu, diced (optional)
- 1/2 cup green beans, thinly sliced
- 1/2 cup green onions (scallions), chopped
- 3 cloves garlic, minced
- 2 Tbsp. soy sauce or tamari
- 1 Tbsp. of vegetarian oyster sauce
- 1/2 Tsp. ground black pepper
- Cooking oil for frying
- Sweet chili sauce or dipping sauce of your choice

Lumpia is a versatile dish, and you can adjust the vegetables and seasonings according to your preference. Feel free to add or substitute other vegetables like bell peppers, mushrooms, or bamboo shoots. Enjoy these delicious and crispy spring rolls!

- In a large skillet or wok, heat a tablespoon of cooking oil over medium heat. Add the minced garlic and sauté until fragrant.
- Add the cabbage, carrots, bean sprouts, tofu (if using), and green beans to the skillet. Stir-fry for about 3-4 minutes until the vegetables are slightly softened.
- Add the soy sauce, oyster sauce , and ground black pepper to the skillet. Stir-fry for another 2-3 minutes until the vegetables are cooked but still crisp.
- Remove the skillet from the heat and let the vegetable mixture cool slightly.
- Take a lumpia wrapper and place it on a flat surface. Spoon about 2 tablespoons of the vegetable mixture onto the lower third of the wrapper.
- Roll the wrapper tightly over the filling, then fold the sides inward, and continue rolling until you have a neat, tight spring roll. Moisten the end of the wrapper with water to seal it.
- Repeat the process with the remaining vegetable mixture and lumpia wrappers until you have used up all the filling.
- Heat cooking oil in a deep pan or pot over medium-high heat. Make sure there is enough oil to fully submerge the spring rolls.
- Carefully place the vegetarian lumpia into the hot oil, seam side down. Fry them in batches until they turn golden brown and crispy, turning them occasionally for even cooking. This typically takes about 5-7 minutes per batch.
- Once cooked, use a slotted spoon or tongs to remove the lumpia from the oil and transfer them to a plate lined with paper towels to drain excess oil.
- Serve the lumpia hot with sweet chili sauce or dipping sauce of your choice.

# Atsara

## INGREDIENTS

- 2 cups green papaya, shredded
- 1/2 cup carrots, julienned
- 1/4 cup red and green bell peppers, thinly sliced
- 2 tbsp raisins
- 1/2 cup white vinegar
- 1/4 cup sugar
- 1/2 tsp salt
- 1 tsp whole peppercorns
- 2 cloves garlic, minced
- 1 small chili (optional, for spice)
- 1/2 cup water

A refreshing and tangy pickled green papaya salad mixed with carrots, bell peppers, and raisins, soaked in a sweet-sour vinegar brine, perfect as a side dish.

- In a bowl, sprinkle a little salt over the shredded papaya and let it sit for 10 minutes. Squeeze out excess liquid and set aside.
- In a saucepan, combine vinegar, sugar, water, salt, peppercorns, and garlic. Bring to a light simmer until the sugar dissolves.
- Remove from heat and let it cool slightly.
- In a jar or container, combine the shredded papaya, carrots, bell peppers, raisins, and optional chili.
- Pour the cooled vinegar mixture over the vegetables, ensuring everything is submerged.
- Cover and refrigerate for at least 24 hours before serving to allow the flavors to develop.

Notes

# Banana Blossom Fritters

## INGREDIENTS

- 2 cups banana blossoms, finely shredded
- 1 small onion, finely chopped
- 2 cloves garlic, minced
- 1/2 cup grated carrots (optional, for color and flavor)
- 1/2 cup all-purpose flour
- 1/4 cup cornstarch (for extra crispiness)
- 1/2 tsp baking powder
- 1 tsp salt
- 1/2 tsp ground black pepper
- 1/2 tsp smoked paprika or chili powder (optional)
- 1 egg (or 2 tbsp flaxseed mixed with 5 tbsp water for a vegan option)
- 1/2 cup water (adjust as needed for batter consistency)
- 1/4 cup chopped parsley or cilantro (optional)
- Cooking oil for frying

Crispy and golden, these banana blossom fritters are a delightful vegetarian snack or appetizer. Made with shredded banana blossoms, herbs, and spices, they're perfect for dipping in your favorite sauce.

- Clean the banana blossoms by removing the tough outer layers and the hard florets. Shred the tender inner parts finely and soak them in water with a little salt or vinegar for 10-15 minutes to remove any bitterness. Rinse well and squeeze out excess water.
- In a large bowl, combine the flour, cornstarch, baking powder, salt, pepper, and paprika (if using). Mix well.
- Add the egg (or flaxseed mixture), water, and mix until a smooth batter forms. Fold in the shredded banana blossoms, onion, garlic, carrots, and parsley.
- Adjust Consistency:
- The mixture should be thick enough to hold together but not too dry. Add a little more water or flour as needed.
- Heat about 1 inch of cooking oil in a deep pan or skillet over medium heat. Test the oil by dropping a small amount of batter; if it sizzles, it's ready.
- Scoop spoonfuls of the mixture and gently drop them into the hot oil. Flatten slightly with the back of a spoon. Fry in batches to avoid overcrowding the pan. Cook for 2-3 minutes per side or until golden brown and crispy.
- Remove the fritters from the oil and drain them on a paper towel-lined plate to remove excess oil.
- Serve warm with your favorite dipping sauces, such as vinegar with chili, sweet chili sauce, or garlic mayo.

# Dumplings

- Filling:
- 1 cup cabbage, finely chopped
- 1/2 cup carrots, grated
- 1/2 cup firm tofu, crumbled
- 1/4 cup mushrooms, chopped
- 2 cloves garlic, minced
- 1/2 onion, chopped
- 1 tbsp soy sauce
- 1/2 tsp sesame oil, salt, pepper, grated ginger
- 1 tbsp cornstarch
- Wrappers (or use store-bought):
- 2 cups flour, 1/2 cup warm water, 1/2 tsp salt
- Dipping Sauce:
- 1/4 cup soy sauce, 2 tbsp vinegar, 1 tsp sugar, 1 tbsp chopped green onions

These dumplings are filled with tofu, vegetables, and seasonings, then pan-fried, steamed, or boiled. Served with a soy-vinegar dipping sauce, they make a perfect appetizer or snack.

- Prepare Dough (if making from scratch) – Mix flour, salt, water, knead, rest 30 min, roll out, cut into circles.
- Make Filling – Sauté garlic, onions, ginger, add vegetables and tofu, season, stir in cornstarch, let cool.
- Assemble – Place filling in wrapper, fold, seal edges.
- Cook –
- Pan-fry: Brown, add water, cover, steam 5 min.
- Steam: 10-12 min.
- Boil: Until they float (about 5 min).
- Dipping Sauce – Mix all ingredients, garnish with green onions.

## Notes

# Siopao

Ingredients: Siopao dough:
- 3 cups all-purpose flour
- 1/4 cup sugar
- 1 Tbsp. baking powder
- 1/2 Tsp. salt
- 2 Tbsp. vegetable oil
- 1 Tbsp. active dry yeast
- 3/4 cup warm water

---

- Ingredients: Asado-style filling:
- 1 1/2 cups tofu diced into small pieces
- 1 cup diced mushroom
- 1/4 cup soy sauce
- 2 Tbsp. hoisin sauce
- 2 Tbsp. tomato ketchup
- 2 Tbsp. brown sugar
- 2 cloves garlic, minced
- 1 onion, finely chopped
- 1 Tbsp. vegetable oil
- 1/4 cup water
- 1 Tbsp. cornstarch (optional, for thickening)

The soft and fluffy steamed buns paired with the savory and sweet filling create a satisfying snack or meal option for vegetarians and those looking to enjoy a meat-free version of this Filipino favorite.

- For the Dough: In a mixing bowl, combine the all-purpose flour, sugar, baking powder, and salt. Mix well.
- In a separate small bowl, dissolve the yeast in warm water. Let it sit for 5 minutes until it becomes foamy.
- Add the yeast mixture and vegetable oil to the dry ingredients. Mix until a soft dough forms.
- Transfer the dough onto a lightly floured surface and knead for about 5-7 minutes until the dough becomes smooth and elastic.
- Place the dough in a greased bowl, cover it with a clean kitchen towel, and let it rise in a warm place for about 1-2 hours or until it doubles in size.

- For the Filling: Heat vegetable oil in a pan over medium heat. Sauté the garlic and onion until fragrant and translucent.
- Add the tofu and mushroom to the pan and cook until slightly browned.
- In a small bowl, whisk together the soy sauce, hoisin sauce, tomato ketchup, brown sugar, water, and cornstarch (if using) until well combined.
- Pour the sauce mixture into the pan with the tofu and mushroom. Stir to coat evenly.
- Reduce the heat to low, cover the pan, and simmer for about 10-15 minutes to allow the flavors to meld together. If the mixture appears too dry, add a little more water.
- Remove the pan from heat and let the vegetarian Asado filling cool.

# Siopao

- "Punch down the risen dough to release the air. Divide the dough into equal-sized pieces, depending on your desired Siopao size. Roll out each dough piece into a circle or oval shape, about 4-5 inches in diameter.
- Place a spoonful of the cooled Asado filling in the center of the dough. Gather the edges of the dough towards the center, pleating and sealing it at the top. Pinch the dough to seal it completely. Repeat the process for the remaining dough and filling.
- Place each assembled Siopao on a small piece of parchment paper and arrange them in a steamer basket, leaving enough space between each Siopao for them to expand. Cover the steamer basket with a clean kitchen towel and let the Siopao rise for another 20-30 minutes.
- Steam the Siopao over high heat for about 15-20 minutes or until the buns are puffed and cooked through. Remove the Siopao from the steamer and let them cool slightly before serving.

## Notes

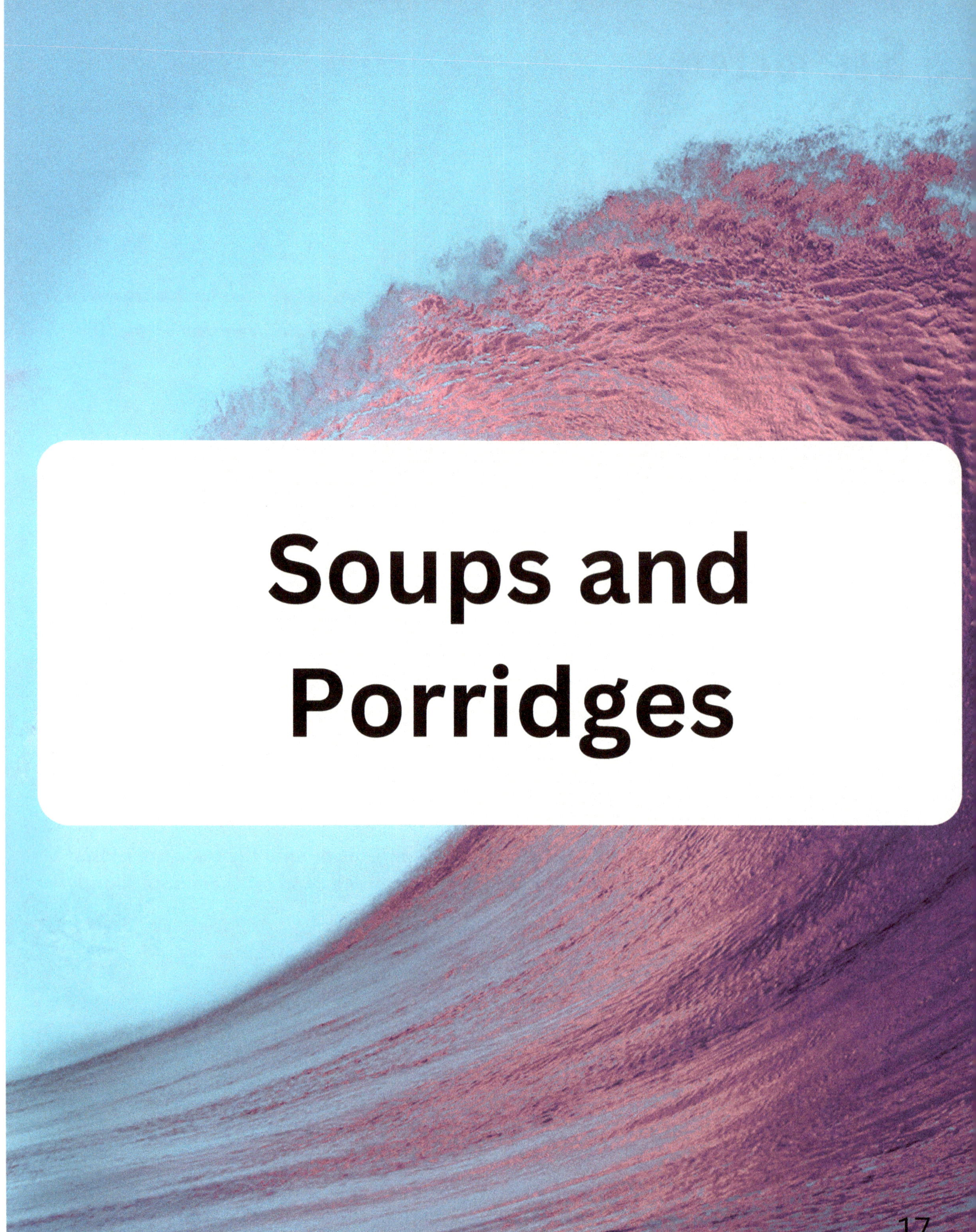

# Soups and Porridges

# Arroz Caldo

## INGREDIENTS

- 1 cup glutinous rice (also known as sticky rice)
- 1/2 cup jasmine rice or long-grain rice
- 4 cups vegetable broth
- 1 cup of soy-based protein or seitan diced
- 1 thumb-sized piece of ginger, peeled and minced
- 4 cloves garlic, minced
- 1 medium-sized onion, chopped
- 2 Tbsp. cooking oil
- 1 Tbsp. soy sauce or tamari
- Salt and pepper to taste
- Toppings:
- Fried garlic
- Sliced spring onions
- Hard-boiled eggs (optional, omit for vegan version)
- Calamansi or lime wedges

Arroz caldo is a comforting and satisfying dish that is perfect for breakfast, brunch, or a nourishing meal any time of the day. Enjoy this vegetarian twist on a classic Filipino favorite!

- In a large pot, heat the cooking oil over medium heat. Add the minced garlic, chopped onion, and minced ginger. Sauté until the onion becomes translucent and the garlic is fragrant.
- Add the vegetarian Protein (such as soy-based chicken or seitan) to the pot and stir-fry for a few minutes until lightly browned.
- Add the glutinous rice and jasmine rice (or long-grain rice) to the pot. Stir well to combine the rice with the other ingredients.
- Pour in the vegetable broth and soy sauce or tamari. Stir everything together to ensure the rice and vegetarian Protein are fully immersed in the broth.
- Bring the mixture to a boil, then reduce the heat to low. Cover the pot and let the arroz caldo simmer for about 30-40 minutes, or until the rice grains are fully cooked and have a porridge-like consistency. Stir occasionally to prevent sticking and to ensure even cooking.
- Season with salt and pepper to taste. Adjust the seasoning according to your preference.
- Remove from heat and serve the arroz caldo hot.
- Garnish each serving with fried garlic, sliced spring onions, and optional toppings such as hard-boiled eggs (omit for vegan version).
- Squeeze calamansi or lime juice over the arroz caldo for a tangy flavor, if desired.

# Champorado

## INGREDIENTS

- 1 cup glutinous rice
- 4 cups water
- 4-5 pieces tablea (Filipino cacao tablets) or 1/2 cup cocoa powder
- 1/2 cup sugar (adjust to taste)
- 1/2 tsp salt
- 1/2 cup evaporated milk or coconut milk (for topping)

Champorado is a rich and creamy Filipino chocolate rice porridge made with glutinous rice and tablea (cacao tablets), served with a swirl of evaporated milk. It's a comforting and indulgent dish, often enjoyed for breakfast or as a snack.

- Cook the Rice – In a pot, bring water to a boil. Add glutinous rice, stir occasionally to prevent sticking, and cook until soft.
- Add Chocolate – Melt tablea or stir in cocoa powder until fully dissolved.
- Sweeten – Add sugar and salt, stirring until well combined. Simmer until thick.
- Serve – Pour into bowls and drizzle with evaporated or coconut milk.

Notes

# Lomi

## INGREDIENTS

- 250g fresh lomi noodles (or thick egg noodles)
- 4 cups vegetable broth or water
- 1 tbsp cooking oil
- 1 small onion, chopped
- 3 cloves garlic, minced
- 1 small carrot, julienned
- 1/2 cup cabbage, shredded
- 1/4 cup bell pepper, sliced
- 1/2 cup mushrooms, sliced
- 2 tbsp soy sauce
- 1 tbsp oyster sauce (or vegetarian alternative)
- 1 tsp salt
- 1/2 tsp black pepper
- 1 tbsp cornstarch mixed with 2 tbsp water (for thickening)
- 1 egg, beaten (optional, for a richer broth)
- Green onions, fried garlic, and calamansi (for garnish)

Lomi is a comforting Filipino noodle soup known for its thick, savory broth and chewy egg noodles. This hearty dish is packed with vegetables and seasonings, making it a satisfying meal on its own.

- Heat oil in a pot over medium heat. Sauté onion and garlic until fragrant.
- Add mushrooms, carrots, and bell peppers. Stir-fry for 2 minutes.
- Pour in the vegetable broth and bring to a boil. Add soy sauce, oyster sauce, salt, and pepper.
- Add the fresh lomi noodles and simmer for 3-5 minutes until tender.
- Stir in the cornstarch slurry and mix until the broth thickens.
- Slowly drizzle in the beaten egg while stirring to create egg ribbons (optional).
- Add shredded cabbage and simmer for 1 more minute. Adjust seasoning to taste.
- Serve hot, garnished with green onions, fried garlic, and a squeeze of calamansi.

Notes

# Tinola

## INGREDIENTS

- 1 block firm tofu, cubed
- 2 Tbsp. cooking oil
- 1 onion, chopped
- 3 cloves garlic, minced
- 1 thumb-sized ginger, sliced
- 2 green papayas or chayote, peeled and cut into wedges
- 4 cups vegetable broth
- 2 cups water
- 1 bunch spinach
- Salt and pepper to taste
- Sliced chili pepper (optional, for added heat)

Vegetarian tinola is a nourishing and flavorful soup that combines the freshness of vegetables with the comforting warmth of ginger-infused broth. It's a perfect dish to enjoy on chilly days or when you're in need of a comforting and healthy meal.

- Heat the cooking oil in a pot over medium heat. Add the cubed tofu and fry until golden brown. Remove the tofu from the pot and set it aside.
- In the same pot, sauté the onion, garlic, and ginger until fragrant and translucent.
- Add the green papayas or chayote wedges to the pot and cook for a few minutes, stirring occasionally.
- Pour in the vegetable broth and water. Bring the liquid to a boil, then reduce the heat to a simmer and let it cook until the papayas or chayote are tender.
- Add the fried tofu back into the pot and simmer for a few more minutes to allow the flavors to blend.
- Stir in the spinach and cook until they are wilted.
- Season the soup salt, and pepper according to your taste. Adjust the seasoning as needed.
- If you prefer a spicy kick, add some sliced chili pepper to the soup.
- Once everything is cooked and seasoned to your liking, remove the pot from the heat.
- Serve the vegetarian tinola hot and enjoy it with steamed rice.

Notes

# Sinigang

## INGREDIENTS

- 8 cups vegetable broth
- 1 medium-sized onion, quartered
- 2 medium-sized tomatoes, quartered
- 1 medium-sized daikon radish, peeled and sliced
- 1 medium-sized eggplant, sliced
- 1 bunch spinach, leaves separated from the stems
- 1 cup green beans, trimmed and cut into bite-sized pieces
- 1 cup okra, ends trimmed
- 2-3 pieces green chili peppers, optional for spice
- 2 Tbsp. tamarind paste or 4-5 pieces fresh tamarind pods
- Salt and pepper to taste
- Fresh cilantro or scallions, chopped (for garnish)
- Steamed rice (for serving)

SInigang is a comforting and flavorful soup that highlights the natural goodness of vegetables. It's a popular dish in Filipino cuisine, and this vegetarian version allows you to enjoy its delightful flavors without the meat.

- In a large pot, bring the vegetable broth to a boil over medium heat.
- If using fresh tamarind pods, place them in a bowl with hot water and let them soak for a few minutes. Once softened, extract the pulp by pressing and straining it through a sieve. Discard the seeds and fibers, and set aside the tamarind pulp. If using tamarind paste, dissolve it in a cup of warm water and set it aside.
- Add the quartered onion and tomatoes to the boiling broth. Let them simmer for about 5 minutes to release their flavors.
- Add the sliced daikon radish, eggplant, green beans, and okra to the pot. Cook for about 5-8 minutes, or until the vegetables are tender.
- Stir in the tamarind pulp or tamarind paste mixture. Season with salt, and pepper to taste. Adjust the seasoning according to your preference.
- Add the kangkong leaves or spinach and green chili peppers (if using). Let them cook for a few minutes until wilted.
- Remove the pot from the heat and let it rest for a few minutes to allow the flavors to meld together.
- Serve the sinigang hot in bowls, garnished with fresh cilantro or scallions.
- Enjoy the sinigang with steamed rice on the side.

# Bulalo

## INGREDIENTS

6 cups vegetable broth
1 corn on the cob, cut into chunks
1 large potato, quartered
1 cup mushrooms (shiitake or king oyster), thickly sliced
1/2 small cabbage, quartered
1 bunch bok choy
1 small onion, quartered
1 tbsp soy sauce
1 tbsp black peppercorns
Salt to taste

A rich and hearty Filipino clear soup with a flavorful plant-based broth, loaded with corn, bok choy, napa cabbage, and thick-cut mushrooms as a meat alternative.

- In a large pot, bring the vegetable broth to a boil.
- Add the onion, corn, potato, and mushrooms. Let simmer for 15 minutes.
- Stir in soy sauce and black peppercorns, then continue simmering for another 10 minutes.
- Add the cabbage and bok choy and cook for another 5 minutes until tender.
- Season with salt to taste and serve hot.

Notes

23

Main Dishes

# Pochero

## INGREDIENTS

- 1 tbsp cooking oil
- 1 small onion, chopped
- 1 small tomato, chopped
- 1 cup vegetable broth
- 1/2 block firm tofu, cubed and fried
- 1 cup potatoes, diced
- 1 saba banana, sliced
- 1/2 cup chickpeas
- 1/2 small cabbage, quartered
- 1 tbsp tomato paste
- 1 tsp soy sauce
- Salt and black pepper to taste

A hearty and slightly sweet Filipino tomato-based stew, filled with chickpeas, potatoes, saba bananas, cabbage, and tofu for a delicious plant-based twist.

- Heat oil in a pot and sauté onions and tomatoes until softened.
- Add the tomato paste, soy sauce, and vegetable broth, stirring well.
- Stir in potatoes and let simmer for 10 minutes.
- Add saba bananas, chickpeas, and fried tofu. Cook for another 5 minutes.
- Add the cabbage and let simmer for 3 more minutes.
- Season with salt and black pepper, then serve hot with steamed rice.

Notes

# Dinuguan

## INGREDIENTS

- 1 cup mushrooms (shiitake or button), finely chopped
- 1/2 block firm tofu, diced
- 1 cup vegetable broth
- 1/2 cup black beans, blended into a smooth paste (as a blood alternative)
- 1 tbsp soy sauce
- 1 small onion, chopped
- 1 tbsp vinegar
- 1 tsp black pepper
- 1 green chili pepper, sliced
- 1 tbsp cooking oil
- Salt to taste

A bold and savory Filipino dark stew, made with a rich, umami-packed plant-based sauce using mushrooms and tofu instead of pork, served with steamed rice.

- Heat oil in a pan and sauté onions until translucent.
- Add mushrooms and tofu, cooking until slightly browned.
- Pour in the vegetable broth, blended black beans, and soy sauce, then bring to a simmer.
- Stir in vinegar, black pepper, and chili peppers, cooking for another 5 minutes.
- Season with salt and serve hot with steamed rice.

Notes

# Pinakbet

## INGREDIENTS

- 1 medium-sized bitter melon (ampalaya), seeds and pith removed, sliced
- 1 medium-sized eggplant, sliced
- 1 medium-sized squash, peeled and cubed
- 1 cup long beans (sitaw), cut into 2-inch pieces
- 2 medium-sized tomatoes, chopped
- 1 medium-sized onion, chopped
- 4 cloves garlic, minced
- 2 Tbsp. vegetarian oyster sauce
- 2 cups water or vegetable broth
- 2 Tbsp. cooking oil
- Salt and pepper to taste

Pinakbet is a versatile dish, and you can modify the vegetable combination based on what is available and to suit your preferences. Some variations include adding okra, green papaya, or adding additional spices like ginger or chili for added heat. Enjoy the rich flavors of this classic Filipino dish!

- Heat the cooking oil in a large pot or wok over medium heat.
- Sauté the minced garlic until fragrant and golden brown.
- Add the onions and tomatoes to the pot and cook until the tomatoes have softened.
- Stir in the vegetarian oyster sauce for flavors.
- Add the bitter melon (ampalaya), eggplant, squash, and long beans to the pot. Stir gently to coat the vegetables with the sauce mixture.
- Pour in the water or vegetable broth, cover the pot, and let it simmer for about 15-20 minutes, or until the vegetables are tender but still retain their shape.
- Season with salt and pepper to taste.
- Once the vegetables are cooked to your desired tenderness, remove the pot from the heat.
- Serve the pinakbet hot with steamed rice.

Notes

# Chop Seuy

## INGREDIENTS

- 2 Tbsp. cooking oil
- 1 medium-sized onion, thinly sliced
- 3 cloves garlic, minced
- 1 cup broccoli florets
- 1 cup cauliflower florets
- 1 cup carrots, julienned or thinly sliced
- 1 cup bell peppers, thinly sliced
- 1 cup cabbage, shredded
- 1 cup snow peas or sugar snap peas
- 1 cup mushrooms, sliced
- 1 cup tofu, diced (optional)
- 2 Tbsp. soy sauce or tamari
- 1 Tbsp. vegetarian oyster sauce
- 1 cup vegetable broth or water
- 1 Tbsp. cornstarch (optional, for thickening the sauce)
- Salt and pepper to taste
- Cooked rice or noodles for serving

Vegetarian chop suey is a versatile dish, and you can customize it by adding or substituting vegetables based on your taste. You can also adjust the seasoning and sauce to suit your preference. Enjoy this flavorful and nutritious  chop suey!

- Heat the cooking oil in a large wok or skillet over medium heat.
- Add the sliced onion and minced garlic to the pan. Sauté until the onion becomes translucent and the garlic is fragrant.
- Add the broccoli, cauliflower, carrots, bell peppers, cabbage, snow peas, mushrooms, and tofu (if using) to the pan. Stir-fry for a few minutes until the vegetables start to soften but still retain their crispness.
- In a small bowl, mix together the soy sauce and oyster sauce. Pour the sauce mixture over the vegetables in the pan. Stir well to coat the vegetables evenly.
- Add the vegetable broth or water to the pan. Cover and let the vegetables simmer for a few minutes until they are cooked to your desired tenderness.
- If you prefer a thicker sauce, dissolve the cornstarch in a small amount of water to make a slurry. Add the slurry to the pan and stir until the sauce thickens.
- Taste the chopsuey and season with salt and pepper according to your preference.
- Remove from heat and serve the vegetarian chopsuey hot over cooked rice or noodles.

# Dinengdeng

## INGREDIENTS

- 4 cups vegetable broth
- 5 pieces okra, sliced
- 1 small eggplant, sliced
- 1/2 cup string beans, cut into 2-inch pieces
- 1/2 cup bitter melon, sliced
- 1 medium tomato, chopped
- 1 tbsp soy sauce
- 1 tsp miso paste (optional for umami)
- Salt and black pepper to taste

A light and nourishing Filipino vegetable stew, featuring okra, eggplant, string beans, and bitter melon in a simple plant-based broth.

- In a pot, bring the vegetable broth to a gentle boil.
- Add the chopped tomatoes and simmer for 5 minutes.
- Stir in the soy sauce and miso paste, mixing well.
- Add okra, eggplant, string beans, and bitter melon, then let simmer for 10 minutes.
- Season with salt and black pepper to taste.
- Serve hot with steamed rice.

## Notes

# Inon-unan

## INGREDIENTS

- 2 cups sliced eggplant, cut into chunks
- 1 medium onion, sliced
- 4 cloves garlic, minced
- 2 tbsp ginger, julienned
- 1/4 cup vinegar (preferably coconut or cane vinegar)
- 1/4 cup water
- 2 tbsp soy sauce (optional for additional umami)
- 1 tsp black peppercorns
- 2 pieces bay leaves
- 2 green chilies, sliced
- Salt to taste
- 2 tbsp cooking oil

Inon-unan is a classic Filipino dish known for its tangy and savory flavors, achieved by braising vegetables in a mixture of vinegar, ginger, garlic, and onions. This dish is simple yet satisfying, offering a balance of sour and savory that pairs perfectly with steamed rice.

- Wash the eggplant thoroughly. Cut into bite-sized chunks and set aside.
- Heat cooking oil in a pan over medium heat. Sauté the onion, garlic, and ginger until fragrant.
- Arrange the eggplant in the pan over the sautéed aromatics. Add the black peppercorns, bay leaves, and green chilie
- Pour in the vinegar and water. Avoid stirring to let the vinegar cook properly and to prevent a raw vinegar taste.
- Cover the pan and let the mixture simmer over low heat for 15-20 minutes or until the vegetables are tender and the flavors are well incorporated. If using soy sauce, add it halfway through the cooking process.
- Taste and adjust the seasoning with salt as needed. Add more water if you prefer a lighter sauce.
- Transfer the Inon-unan to a serving dish. Garnish with additional chilies if desired.

Notes

# Paklay

## INGREDIENTS

- 2 cups vegetarian protein (such as seitan, tofu, or tempeh), slice into stripe
- 1 cup mushrooms, sliced
- 1 cup Pineapple stripes
- 1 cup black beans
- 1 cup bamboo shoots, sliced
- 1 medium-sized onion, chopped
- Small size ginger, grated
- Red Bellpepper, julienned
- 3 cloves garlic, minced
- 2 Tbsp. cooking oil
- 2 Tbsp. soy sauce or tamari
- 2 Tbsp. vinegar (preferably cane vinegar or white vinegar)
- 1 Tbsp. brown sugar or sweetener of your choice
- 1 Tbsp. tamarind paste (sampalok)
- 1 cup vegetable broth or water
- Salt and pepper to taste
- 5pcs Bay leaves

Feel free to customize the recipe by adding or substituting other vegetables based on your taste. Enjoy this vegetarian version of a Filipino classic!

- In a large pot or deep skillet, heat the cooking oil over medium heat. Add the grated ginger, minced garlic and chopped onion. Sauté until the onion becomes translucent, and the garlic and ginger is fragrant.
- Add the vegetarian protein (such as seitan, tofu, or tempeh) to the pot and stir-fry for a few minutes until lightly browned.
- Add the mushrooms, Pineapple, black beans, bamboo shoots to the pot, red Bellpepper, and bay leaves. Stir everything together.
- In a small bowl, combine the soy sauce or tamari, vinegar, brown sugar or sweetener, tamarind paste, and vegetable broth or water. Mix well to create the sauce.
- Pour the sauce mixture into the pot, ensuring that the vegetables and protein are well coated. Stir gently to combine.
- Bring the mixture to a boil, then reduce the heat to low. Cover the pot and let the Paklay simmer for about 15-20 minutes, or until the vegetables are tender and the flavors have melded together.
- Taste and adjust the seasoning as needed, adding more salt, pepper, or sugar according to your preference.
- Remove from heat and serve the Paklay hot with steamed rice.

# Ginisang Gulay

## INGREDIENTS

- 1 medium-sized eggplant, cut into cubes
- 1 medium-sized squash, cut into cubes
- 1 cup chopped string beans/green beans
- 1 medium-sized onion, chopped
- 4 cloves garlic, minced
- 2 tbsp cooking oil
- 1/2 cup vegetable broth
- 1 tbsp soy sauce
- Salt and pepper to taste

You can also add other vegetables such as string beans, okra, bitter melon, coyote, pumpkin or bok choy. Feel free to adjust the seasoning and the amount of vegetable broth according to your taste preference. Enjoy!

- In a large pan or wok, heat the cooking oil over medium-high heat.
- Add the chopped onion and minced garlic. Sauté until fragrant and slightly golden brown.
- Add the eggplant, string beans, and squash. Sauté for 3-4 minutes until they start to soften.
- Add the vegetable broth and soy sauce. Mix well.
- Cover the pan or wok and let it simmer for 8-10 minutes or until the vegetables are tender.
- Season with salt and pepper to taste.
- Serve hot with rice.

## Notes

# Adobo

## INGREDIENTS

- 1 cup firm tofu, cubed
- 1 cup tempeh, cubed
- 1/2 cup soy sauce or tamari
- 1/2 cup vinegar (preferably cane vinegar or white vinegar)
- 1/2 cup water
- 4 cloves garlic, minced
- 1 Tsp. whole peppercorns
- 2 bay leaves
- 2 Tbsp. cooking oil
- Salt to taste
- Optional: 1 tablespoon brown sugar or sweetener of your choice for a slightly sweeter adobo

Vegetarian adobo is a savory and flavorful dish that combines the tanginess of vinegar and the richness of soy sauce. Feel free to experiment with additional vegetables or protein sources like mushrooms or seitan. Enjoy this meatless twist on a classic Filipino favorite!

- In a bowl, combine the soy sauce or tamari, vinegar, water, minced garlic, peppercorns, and bay leaves. Mix well to create the adobo marinade.
- Place the tofu and tempeh cubes in a shallow dish or ziplock bag. Pour the adobo marinade over the tofu and tempeh, ensuring they are fully coated. Let them marinate for at least 30 minutes, or preferably overnight in the refrigerator.
- Heat the cooking oil in a large pan or skillet over medium heat. Remove the tofu and tempeh cubes from the marinade, reserving the marinade for later.
- Add the tofu and tempeh to the pan and cook until lightly browned on all sides. Remove them from the pan and set aside.
- In the same pan, add the reserved marinade and bring it to a boil. Reduce the heat to low and let it simmer for a few minutes.
- Return the tofu and tempeh to the pan and simmer in the marinade for about 10-15 minutes, allowing the flavors to meld and the tofu and tempeh to absorb the sauce.
- Taste and adjust the seasoning as needed. If desired, you can add a tablespoon of brown sugar or sweetener to slightly sweeten the adobo.
- Remove the bay leaves before serving. Serve the vegetarian adobo hot with steamed rice.

# Humbang Langka

- 3 cups unripe jackfruit, peeled and cut into bite-sized chunks
- 3 tbsp cooking oil
- 1 medium onion, chopped
- 5 cloves garlic, minced
- 2 tbsp ginger, julienned
- 1/4 cup soy sauce
- 1/4 cup vinegar
- 1/4 cup water or vegetable broth
- 2 tbsp brown sugar (adjust to taste)
- 1 tsp black peppercorns
- 2 pieces bay leaves
- 1/2 cup pineapple chunks (optional, for a sweet twist)
- Salt to taste
- Chopped scallions and red chili for garnish

Humbang Langka is a flavorful Filipino dish featuring tender unripe jackfruit braised in a savory and tangy soy sauce and vinegar mixture, enriched with garlic, onions, and a hint of sweetness. It's a delicious and hearty vegetarian alternative to the classic pork humba.

- Wash the unripe jackfruit thoroughly. Peel and cut it into bite-sized pieces.
- Heat the cooking oil in a pan over medium heat. Sauté the onion, garlic, and ginger until fragrant and translucent.
- Add the jackfruit pieces and sauté for 5 minutes to coat them in the aromatics.
- Pour in the soy sauce, vinegar, and water or vegetable broth. Add the brown sugar, black peppercorns, and bay leaves. Stir gently to combine.
- Cover the pan and let the mixture simmer over low heat for 25-30 minutes or until the jackfruit is tender and has absorbed the flavors. Add the pineapple chunks if desired and cook for an additional 5 minutes.
- Taste the sauce and adjust the salt and sweetness to your preference.
- Transfer the Humbang Langka to a serving dish. Garnish with chopped scallions and red chili for a pop of color and spice.

## Notes

# Kare-Kare

## INGREDIENTS

- 2 cups vegetarian protein (such as tofu, tempeh, or seitan), cubed
- 1 cup eggplant, sliced
- 1 cup green beans, cut into 2-inch pieces
- 1 cup bok choy or spinach, chopped
- 1 cup baby corn, halved
- 1 cup peanut butter (preferably unsweetened)
- 4 cups vegetable broth or water
- 1 medium-sized onion, chopped
- 3 cloves garlic, minced
- 2 Tbsp. cooking oil
- 2 Tbsp. soy sauce or tamari
- 1 Tbsp. annatto powder (achuete)
- 1 Tbsp. rice flour or cornstarch (for thickening)
- Salt and pepper to taste

Kare-Kare is a hearty and flavorful dish that showcases the richness of the peanut sauce and the variety of vegetables. Enjoy this meatless twist on a classic Filipino favorite!

- Heat oil in a pot over medium heat and sauté garlic and onion until fragrant.
- Add tofu, tempeh, or seitan and stir-fry until lightly browned.
- Dissolve annatto powder in warm water and stir it into the pot with soy sauce.
- Pour in vegetable broth, bring to a boil, then reduce heat and simmer for 15-20 minutes.
- Stir in eggplant, green beans, baby corn, and bok choy, then simmer for another 10-15 minutes until tender.
- Mix peanut butter with a ladle of broth until smooth, then stir it into the pot and simmer for 5-10 minutes.
- Whisk rice flour or cornstarch with water, then slowly add to the pot, stirring continuously until thickened.
- Adjust salt and pepper to taste. Serve hot with steamed rice.

Notes

# Tortang Talong



- 4 medium-sized Eggplants
- 4 large eggs
- 1/4 cup all-purpose flour
- Salt and Pepper, to taste
- Cooking oil, for frying

Tortang Talong is a Popular dish in the Philippines that is made from roasted eggplants that are mashed and then friend with an egg coating. Here is a simple recipe for Tortang Talong.

- Roast the Eggplants over an open flame until the skin is charred and the Eggplant is soft. This can be done over a gas stove or grill.
- Once the Eggplants are cool enough to handle, peel off the charred skin and mash the flesh.
- In a bowl, beat the eggs and the mashed Eggplant, flour, salt, and pepper. Mix well.
- Heat a frying pan over medium heat and add enough oil to cover the bottom of the pan.
- Use a spoon to scoop out a portion of the Eggplant mixture and place it into the frying pan. Flatten it out with the back of the spoon to form a patty. Repeat until all the mixture has been used.
- Fry each patty until the bottom is golden brown, then flip over and fry the other side until golden brown.
- Serve the Tortang Talong hot with rice and your choice of dipping sauce. I hope you enjoy this recipe!

Notes

# Ginataang Monggo

## INGREDIENTS

- 1 cup mung beans (monggo), soaked overnight and drained
- 1 can (13.5 oz.) coconut milk
- 2 cups vegetable broth or water
- 1 Tbsp. cooking oil
- 1 medium-sized onion, chopped
- 3 cloves garlic, minced
- 1 medium-sized tomato, chopped
- 1 cup spinach or moringa leaves
- 1 cup squash or pumpkin, diced
- 1 cup eggplant, diced
- Salt and pepper to taste
- Optional toppings:
- Sliced green onions or chives

Ginataang monggo is a comforting and satisfying dish that showcases the creaminess of coconut milk and the earthy flavors of mung beans and vegetables. Enjoy this delightful Filipino dish as a nutritious and hearty meal!

- Heat the cooking oil in a large pot or deep skillet over medium heat. Add the chopped onion and minced garlic. Sauté until the onion becomes translucent and the garlic is fragrant.
- Add the chopped tomato to the pot and cook for a few minutes until softened.
- Add the soaked and drained mung beans to the pot. Stir everything together to combine.
- Pour in the coconut milk and vegetable broth or water. Stir well to fully incorporate the ingredients.
- Bring the mixture to a boil, then reduce the heat to low. Cover the pot and let the ginataang monggo simmer for about 30-40 minutes, or until the mung beans are tender and cooked through. Stir occasionally to prevent sticking and to ensure even cooking.
- Add the diced squash or pumpkin and eggplant to the pot. Stir gently to combine. Continue to simmer for another 10-15 minutes until the vegetables are tender.
- Add the spinach  leaves to the pot. Stir until the leaves wilt and become incorporated into the dish.
- Season with salt and pepper to taste. Adjust the seasoning according to your preference.
- Remove from heat and serve the vegetarian ginataang monggo hot. You can enjoy it as it is or serve it with steamed rice.
- Optional: Top with sliced green onions or chives for added freshness

# Sinantomas

## INGREDIENTS

- 2lbs meatless alternative(plant-based)
- 1/2 cup pineapple juice
- 1/4 cup soy sauce
- 1/2 Tsp. salt
- Oil
- 10 Marble Potatoes
- 4 Cloves garlic (minced)
- 1 medium onion (chopped)
- 5 tomatoes (chopped)
- 2 Tbsp. Ketchup
- 1 cup water
- 1/4 cup grated cheese
- 1/2 cup green peas
- Vegan oyster sauce/ salt
- 1 small red Bell pepper

A creamy Filipino stew with tomato and coconut milk, featuring tender protein, potatoes, peas, and carrots. Perfect for festive meals.

- First, Mix the pineapple juice, soy sauce, and 1/2 tsp salt. Use it to Marinate the plant-based meat for an hour. Then set aside.
- Second, heat oil in a pan and fry some few marble potatoes until it become light brown.  Set aside. Then fry the Marinated plant-based meat.(Reserve the marinade) Set aside.
- Third, Saute the garlic until golden brown, then add the onion and tomato.  Crush while sautéing. And then add the  meat, Ketchup, and the reserved marinade. Stir to combine. Add 1 cup of water and simmer for 5 minutes.
- Next, add potato  and simmer for another 5 minutes.
- Then lastly, add the grated cheese, green peas, and oyster sauce/salt, and small red Bellpepper. Stir. Then ready to serve.

## Notes

# Sisig

## INGREDIENTS

- 1 block firm tofu, pressed and drained and 2 cups mushrooms (such as oyster mushrooms or king oyster mushrooms), sliced
- 1 small onion, finely chopped
- 3 cloves garlic, minced
- 1 red chili pepper, minced (adjust according to your spice preference)
- 1/4 cup soy sauce or tamari
- 2 Tbsp. vinegar (preferably cane vinegar or white vinegar)
- 1 Tbsp. liquid smoke (optional, for smoky flavor)
- 1 Tbsp. cooking oil
- 1 Tbsp. mayonnaise (vegan mayo for a vegan version)
- Juice of 1 calamansi or 1 small lime (optional)
- Salt and pepper to taste
- Chopped green onions or chives (for garnish)

Vegetarian sisig is a flavorful and satisfying dish that captures the essence of the original dish while providing a meatless alternative. Enjoy this vegetarian twist on a classic Filipino favorite!

- If using tofu, press it between paper towels or use a tofu press to remove excess moisture. Cut the tofu into small cubes or crumble it into smaller pieces. Slice the mushrooms into thin strips.
- Heat the cooking oil in a large skillet or pan over medium heat. Add the chopped onion and minced garlic. Sauté until the onion becomes translucent and the garlic is fragrant.
- Add the tofu cubes and sliced mushrooms to the pan. Cook until they are lightly browned and have a slightly crispy texture.
- In a small bowl, mix together the soy sauce or tamari, vinegar, and liquid smoke (if using). Pour the sauce mixture over the tofu and mushrooms in the pan. Stir well to coat the ingredients evenly.
- Add the minced chili pepper to the pan and continue cooking for a few more minutes to allow the flavors to meld together.
- Season with salt and pepper to taste. Adjust the seasoning according to your preference.
- Remove the pan from heat and transfer to a serving dish.
- Drizzle the mayonnaise over . Squeeze the calamansi juice or lime juice over the dish (if desired) for a tangy flavor.
- Garnish with chopped green onions or chives.
- Serve the sisig hot as an appetizer or as a main dish with steamed rice or as a filling for tacos or wraps.

39

# Kaldereta

## INGREDIENTS

- 1 cup vegetarian protein of your choice (such as seitan, tofu, or tempeh), diced
- 1 cup potatoes, peeled and cubed
- 1 cup carrots, peeled and cubed
- 1 cup bell peppers, sliced
- 1 cup green peas
- 1 medium-sized onion, chopped
- 3 cloves garlic, minced
- 2 Tbsp. tomato paste
- 1 cup tomato sauce
- 1 cup vegetable broth or water
- 2 Tbsp. cooking oil
- 1 bay leaf
- 1 Tsp. paprika
- 1 Tsp. soy sauce or tamari
- 1 Tsp. brown sugar or sweetener of your choice
- Salt and pepper to taste

Kaldereta is a flavorful and satisfying dish that showcases the rich tomato sauce and hearty vegetables. Enjoy this meatless version of a Filipino classic!

- Heat the cooking oil in a large pot or deep skillet over medium heat. Add the minced garlic and chopped onion. Sauté until the onion becomes translucent and the garlic is fragrant.
- Add the diced vegetarian protein (such as seitan, tofu, or tempeh) to the pot and stir-fry for a few minutes until lightly browned.
- Add the tomato paste to the pot and cook for a minute, stirring constantly.
- Add the potatoes, carrots, bell peppers, green peas, tomato sauce, vegetable broth or water, bay leaf, paprika, soy sauce, brown sugar, salt, and pepper to the pot. Stir everything together until well combined.
- Bring the mixture to a boil, then reduce the heat to low. Cover the pot and let the Kaldereta simmer for about 25-30 minutes, or until the vegetables are tender and the flavors have melded together.
- Taste and adjust the seasoning as needed, adding more salt, pepper, or sugar according to your preference.
- Remove the bay leaf before serving. Serve the Kaldereta hot with steamed rice or bread.

# Menudo

## INGREDIENTS

- 1 cup soy chunks or seitan, rehydrated and diced
- 1 cup carrots, diced
- 1 cup potatoes, diced
- 1/2 cup green peas
- 1/2 cup bell peppers, diced
- 1/2 cup green beans, cut into 1-inch pieces
- 1/2 cup raisins (optional)
- 1/2 cup tomato sauce
- 1 medium-sized onion, chopped
- 3 cloves garlic, minced
- 2 Tbsp. soy sauce
- 1 Tbsp. tomato paste
- 1 Tbsp. vinegar
- 1 Tbsp. brown sugar or sweetener of your choice
- 1 bay leaf
- 1 cup vegetable broth or water
- 2 Tbsp. cooking oil
- Salt and pepper to taste

Menudo is a hearty and satisfying dish that is perfect for gatherings or as a comforting meal. Enjoy the delicious flavors of this meatless version of a Filipino classic!

- Heat the cooking oil in a large pot or deep skillet over medium heat. Add the minced garlic and chopped onion. Sauté until the onion becomes translucent and the garlic is fragrant.
- Add the diced soy chunks or seitan to the pot and stir-fry for a few minutes until lightly browned.
- Add the diced carrots, potatoes, bell peppers, green beans, green peas, and raisins (if using). Stir to combine the ingredients.
- In a small bowl, mix together the tomato sauce, soy sauce, tomato paste, vinegar, brown sugar, salt, and pepper. Pour this mixture over the vegetables in the pot.
- Add the bay leaf and vegetable broth or water to the pot. Stir everything together until well combined.
- Bring the mixture to a boil, then reduce the heat to low. Cover the pot and let the menudo simmer for about 20-25 minutes, or until the vegetables are tender and the flavors have melded together.
- Taste and adjust the seasoning as needed, adding more salt, pepper, or sugar according to your preference.
- Remove the bay leaf before serving. Serve the menudo hot with steamed rice or crusty bread.

# Bicol Express

- 1 block firm tofu, diced and fried
- 1 can (400ml) coconut milk
- 1 tbsp coconut oil
- 1 onion, chopped
- 3 cloves garlic, minced
- 2 tbsp ginger, minced
- 3-4 green and red chili peppers, sliced
- 1 cup string beans, chopped
- 1 tbsp soy sauce
- 1 tsp sugar
- Salt and pepper to taste
- Crispy fried garlic for garnish
- Steamed rice for serving

A creamy and spicy dish made with tofu and string beans simmered in rich coconut milk with chili peppers, giving it the signature heat and depth of flavor.

- Heat coconut oil in a pan and sauté onions, garlic, and ginger until fragrant.
- Add the sliced chili peppers and cook for another minute.
- Pour in the coconut milk and bring to a simmer.
- Stir in the soy sauce, sugar, and string beans. Cook for about 5 minutes.
- Add the fried tofu and let it simmer for another 3-5 minutes until the flavors meld.
- Season with salt and pepper to taste.
- Serve hot, garnished with crispy fried garlic, alongside steamed rice.

Notes

# Laing

## INGREDIENTS

- 3 cups dried taro leaves
- 1 can (400ml) coconut milk
- 1 cup coconut cream
- 1 tbsp coconut oil
- 1 onion, chopped
- 3 cloves garlic, minced
- 2 tbsp ginger, minced
- 3-4 green and red chili peppers, sliced
- 1/2 block firm tofu, diced and fried
- 1 tbsp soy sauce
- 1 tsp sugar
- Salt and pepper to taste
- Crispy garlic bits for garnish
- Steamed rice for serving

A comforting and creamy dish of dried taro leaves cooked in coconut milk, infused with ginger, garlic, and chili, and enhanced with crispy tofu.

- Heat coconut oil in a pan and sauté onions, garlic, and ginger until aromatic.
- Add sliced chili peppers and stir for another minute.
- Pour in the coconut milk and let it simmer.
- Gently add the dried taro leaves without stirring; allow them to absorb the liquid.
- Once the leaves soften, stir in the soy sauce, sugar, and fried tofu.
- Simmer on low heat for about 15-20 minutes until creamy and thickened.
- Pour in the coconut cream and continue to cook for another 5 minutes.
- Season with salt and pepper to taste.
- Serve hot, garnished with crispy garlic bits, alongside steamed rice.

Notes

# Escabichi

## INGREDIENTS

- 4 pieces plant-based fillets or firm tofu slices
- 1 cup all-purpose flour (optional, for coating)
- 1 tsp salt
- 1/2 tsp black pepper
- Cooking oil for frying
- For the Sauce:
- 1/2 cup vinegar
- 1/4 cup sugar
- 1/4 cup ketchup (for color and flavor)
- 1/2 cup water
- 2 tbsp soy sauce
- 1 tbsp cornstarch dissolved in 2 tbsp water
- Vegetables:
- 1 medium onion, sliced
- 1 medium carrot, julienned
- 1 red bell pepper, julienned
- 1 green bell pepper, julienned
- 2 cloves garlic, minced
- 1 thumb-sized ginger, julienned

A sweet and tangy Filipino dish usually featuring fried fish replaced by your favorite plant-based protein, coated in a vibrant sauce made with vinegar, sugar, and vegetables. Perfect for festive meals or everyday dining.

- 1. Prepare the Protein:
- Season the fillets or tofu slices with salt and pepper.
- (Optional) Coat with flour for extra crispiness.
- Heat oil in a frying pan and fry until golden brown. Set aside.
- 2. Make the Sauce:
- In a bowl, combine vinegar, sugar, ketchup, water, and soy sauce. Stir well.
- Heat a separate pan and sauté garlic, ginger, and onion until fragrant.
- Add carrots, red, and green bell peppers. Sauté for 2-3 minutes.
- Pour in the sauce mixture and bring to a boil.
- Add the dissolved cornstarch and stir until the sauce thickens.
- 3. Assemble:
- Place the fried protein on a serving plate.
- Pour the sauce and vegetables over the top.
- Garnish with additional bell peppers or parsley, if desired.

## Notes

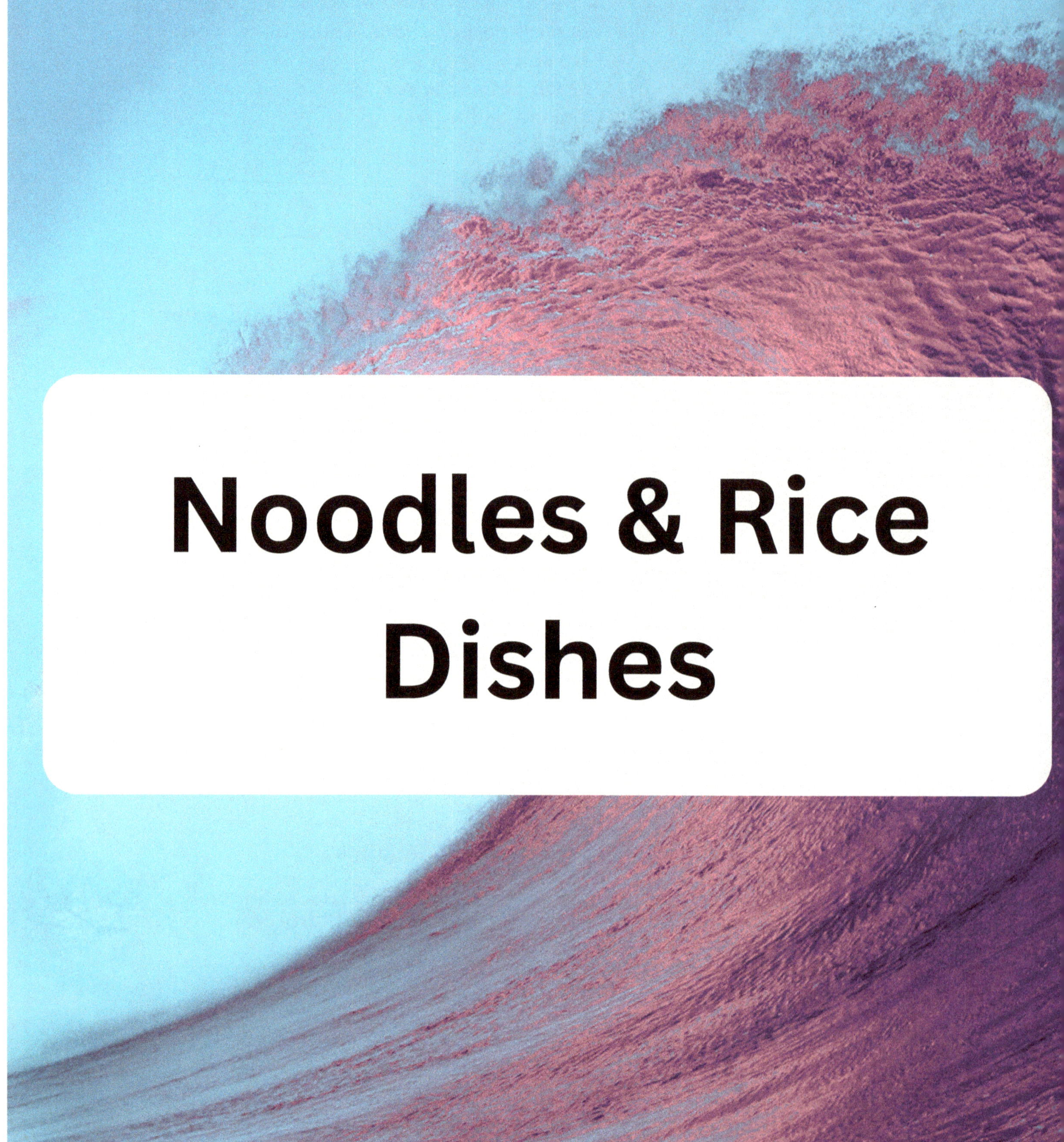


Noodles & Rice
Dishes

# Pancit Bihon

## INGREDIENTS

- 8 ounces (225g) rice noodles (bihon)
- 2 Tbsp. cooking oil
- 1 Tbsp of grated ginger
- 3 cloves garlic, minced
- 1 medium-sized onion, thinly sliced
- 1 cup carrots, julienned or thinly sliced
- 1 cup cabbage, shredded
- 1 cup bell peppers, thinly sliced
- 1 cup snow peas or sugar snap peas
- 1 cup tofu, diced
- 2 Tbsp. soy sauce or tamari
- 2 Tbsp. vegetable broth or water
- 1 Tbsp. vegetarian oyster sauce
- 1 Tbsp. sesame oil
- Salt and pepper to taste
- garnish: sliced green onions, chopped cilantro, or a squeeze of fresh lemon or lime juice

Pancit Bihon is a classic Filipino noodle dish, typically made with rice noodles, vegetables, and sometimes meat or seafood. This flavorful noodle dish is a delicious and satisfying option for vegetarians and noodle lovers alike!

- Prepare the rice noodles according to the package instructions. Drain and set aside.
- In a large pan or wok, heat the cooking oil over medium heat. Add the minced garlic, grated ginger and sliced onion. Sauté until the onion becomes translucent and the garlic is fragrant.
- Add the carrots, cabbage, bell peppers, and snow peas or sugar snap peas to the pan. Stir-fry for a few minutes until the vegetables start to soften but still retain their crispness.
- Push the vegetables to one side of the pan and add the diced tofu to the empty space. Cook the tofu for a few minutes until lightly browned on all sides.
- In a small bowl, mix together the soy sauce or tamari, vegetable broth or water, and oyster sauce. Pour the sauce mixture over the vegetables and tofu. Stir well to combine.
- Add the cooked rice noodles to the pan. Toss and stir-fry everything together, making sure the noodles are evenly coated with the sauce and vegetables are distributed throughout.
- Drizzle the sesame oil over the noodles and continue to stir-fry for a few more minutes until the noodles are heated through.
- Taste and adjust the seasoning with salt and pepper as needed.
- Remove from heat and garnish with sliced green onions, chopped cilantro, or a squeeze of fresh lemon or lime juice, if desired.. Serve the Pancit Bihon hot as a main dish or as a side dish alongside other Filipino favorites.

# Bam-I

## INGREDIENTS

- 100g pancit canton (flour noodles)
- 100g sotanghon (glass noodles), soaked in water until soft
- 2 tbsp cooking oil
- 3 cloves garlic, minced
- 1 small onion, sliced
- 1 small carrot, julienned
- 1/2 cup cabbage, shredded
- 1/4 cup bell pepper, sliced
- 1/2 cup mushrooms, sliced
- 2 tbsp soy sauce
- 1 tbsp oyster sauce (or vegetarian alternative)
- 1/2 tsp black pepper
- 1 tsp salt (adjust to taste)
- 2 cups vegetable broth or water
- 1 tbsp annatto oil (optional, for color)
- Green onions and fried garlic for garnish

Bam-I is a delicious Filipino stir-fried noodle dish that combines pancit canton (flour noodles) and sotanghon (glass noodles) with a medley of vegetables and seasonings. This flavorful, one-pan meal is perfect for any occasion.

- Heat oil in a large pan or wok over medium heat. Sauté garlic and onion until fragrant.
- Add mushrooms, carrots, and bell peppers. Stir-fry for 2 minutes.
- Pour in vegetable broth, soy sauce, oyster sauce, black pepper, and salt. Let it simmer.
- Add pancit canton noodles and cook until slightly tender.
- Stir in sotanghon noodles and let them absorb the broth. Toss everything together until well combined.
- Add cabbage and cook for another minute, ensuring all noodles are fully coated in the sauce.
- Adjust seasoning to taste, then remove from heat.
- Serve hot, garnished with green onions and fried garlic.

## Notes

# Pancit Palabok



- 8 ounces rice noodles (bihon)
- 2 Tbsp. cooking oil
- 1 onion, minced
- 3 cloves garlic, minced
- 2 cups vegetable broth
- 2 Tbsp. soy sauce
- 1 Tbsp. annatto powder (achuete powder), dissolved in 2 Tbsp. water
- 1/2 cup tofu, diced
- 1 cup vegetarian protein (such as textured vegetable protein or soy-based ground meat)
- Salt and pepper to taste
- Toppings:
- Crushed vegetarian chicharon
- Fried tofu, diced
- Boiled eggs, sliced
- Chopped scallions or green onions
- Sliced lemon or calamansi

Pancit Palabok is a delightful and colorful noodle dish that is loved for its distinct flavors. With the substitution of vegetarian-friendly ingredients, you can still enjoy the essence of this traditional Filipino dish.

- Cook the rice noodles (bihon) according to the package instructions. Drain and set aside.
- Heat the cooking oil in a large pan or wok over medium heat. Add the minced onion and garlic, and sauté until fragrant and translucent.
- Stir in the vegetable broth, soy sauce, and annatto powder mixture. Bring to a simmer.
- Add the diced tofu and vegetarian Protein to the pan. Stir well to combine. Cook for about 5 minutes, or until the tofu and vegetarian meat are heated through.
- Season the sauce with salt and pepper to taste. Adjust the seasoning according to your preference.
- Arrange the cooked rice noodles on a serving platter.
- Pour the sauce over the rice noodles, ensuring they are well coated.
- Garnish the Pancit Palabok with crushed vegetarian chicharon, fried tofu, sliced boiled eggs, chopped scallions, and a squeeze of lemon or calamansi.
- Serve the Pancit Palabok immediately, and enjoy!

# Fried Rice

## INGREDIENTS

- 3 cups cooked rice (preferably day-old)
- 2 tbsp cooking oil
- 4 cloves garlic, minced
- 1 small onion, chopped
- 1/2 cup carrots, diced
- 1/2 cup green peas
- 1/2 cup corn kernels
- 1/4 cup bell peppers, diced
- 2 tbsp soy sauce
- 1 tbsp vegetarian oyster sauce (optional)
- 1/2 tsp black pepper
- 1/2 tsp salt (adjust to taste)
- 1/4 tsp turmeric (optional, for color)
- 1/2 tsp sesame oil (optional, for added flavor)
- Green onions for garnish

Filipino-style fried rice is a simple yet flavorful dish, often made with garlic, soy sauce, and vegetables. This vegetarian version is packed with texture and umami, making it a perfect side or main dish.

- Heat oil in a pan over medium heat. Sauté garlic until golden and fragrant.
- Add onions, carrots, and bell peppers. Stir-fry for 2 minutes until slightly softened.
- Add green peas and corn, then stir in soy sauce, vegetarian oyster sauce, black pepper, and salt.
- Increase heat and add the cooked rice, breaking up any clumps while stirring continuously.
- Stir-fry everything for 3-5 minutes until well combined and heated through.
- Drizzle sesame oil for added aroma, then mix well.
- Serve hot, garnished with chopped green onions.

Notes

49

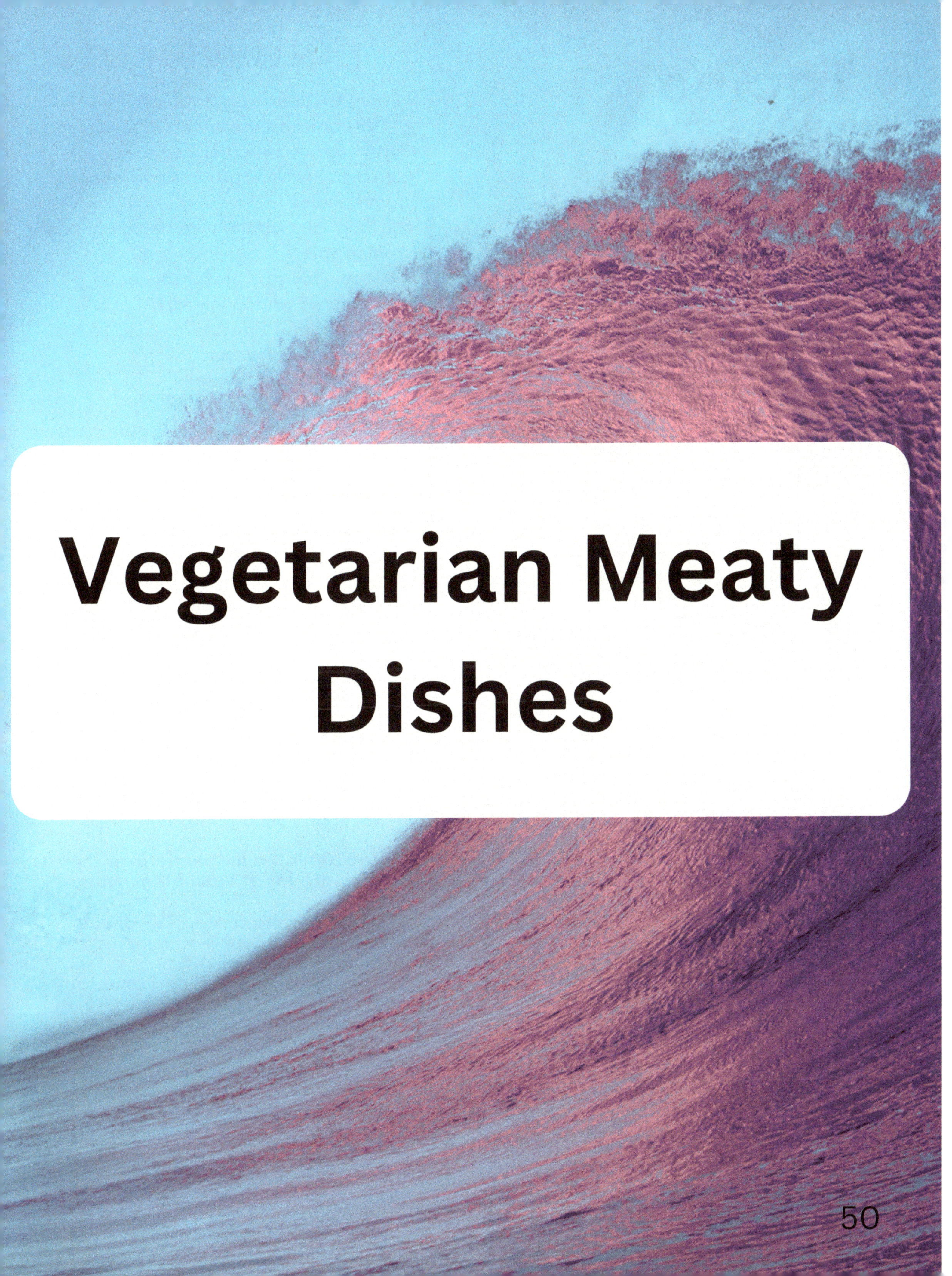
Vegetarian Meaty Dishes

# Tocino

## INGREDIENTS

- 1 cup textured vegetable protein (TVP) or firm tofu, crumbled or sliced
- 1/4 cup soy sauce or tamari
- 2 Tbsp. brown sugar or sweetener of your choice
- 2 Tbsp. pineapple juice (from canned pineapple)
- 1 Tbsp. vinegar (preferably cane vinegar or white vinegar)
- 1 Tbsp. tomato paste
- 1 Tsp. garlic powder
- 1/2 Tsp. onion powder
- 1/2 Tsp. smoked paprika
- 1/4 Tsp. ground black pepper
- 2 Tbsp. cooking oil

Feel free to adjust the sweetness or seasonings according to your taste preferences. Enjoy this meatless twist on a classic Filipino favorite!

- In a bowl, combine the soy sauce or tamari, brown sugar, pineapple juice, vinegar, tomato paste, garlic powder, onion powder, smoked paprika, and black pepper. Mix well to create the marinade.
- If using textured vegetable protein (TVP), rehydrate it according to the package instructions. If using tofu, pat it dry with a paper towel and slice it into thin strips or crumble it into smaller pieces.
- Place the TVP or tofu in a shallow dish or ziplock bag. Pour the marinade over the TVP or tofu, ensuring that all pieces are coated. Marinate for at least 30 minutes, or preferably overnight in the refrigerator.
- Heat the cooking oil in a skillet over medium heat. Add the marinated TVP or tofu, along with any remaining marinade, to the skillet. Cook for about 8-10 minutes, stirring occasionally, until the TVP or tofu is browned and caramelized.
- Serve the vegetarian tocino hot with garlic fried rice and a side of sliced tomatoes or atchara (pickled vegetables).

## Notes

# Embutido

## INGREDIENTS

- 1 cup textured vegetable protein (TVP) or soy protein crumbles
- 1 cup vegetable broth or water, hot
- 1 cup breadcrumbs
- 1/2 cup carrots, finely diced
- 1/2 cup green bell pepper, finely diced
- 1/2 cup red bell pepper, finely diced
- 1/2 cup sweet pickle relish
- 1/4 cup raisins
- 1/4 cup tomato sauce
- 2 Tbsp. soy sauce
- 2 Tbsp. nutritional yeast (optional, for added flavor)
- 1 Tbsp. ground flaxseed mixed with 3 Tbsp. water (flax egg substitute)
- 1 Tbsp. garlic powder
- 1 Tsp. onion powder
- 1/2 Tsp. ground black pepper
- 1/2 Tsp. salt
- Cooking oil, for greasing

Embutido is a flavorful and satisfying dish that can be enjoyed as a main course or as part of a festive spread. It offers a plant-based twist on the traditional Filipino meatloaf, to savor its delicious flavors.

- In a bowl, rehydrate the textured vegetable protein (TVP) or soy protein crumbles by pouring hot vegetable broth or water over them. Let it sit for about 5 minutes until the TVP or soy protein has absorbed the liquid and softened.
- In a large mixing bowl, combine the rehydrated TVP or soy protein, breadcrumbs, carrots, green bell pepper, red bell pepper, sweet pickle relish, raisins, tomato sauce, soy sauce, nutritional yeast (if using), flaxseed mixture, garlic powder, onion powder, black pepper, and salt. Mix well until all the ingredients are evenly combined.
- Preheat the oven to 350°F (175°C).
- Grease a loaf pan or line it with parchment paper.
- Spoon the embutido mixture into the prepared loaf pan, pressing it down firmly to pack it.
- Cover the loaf pan with aluminum foil and bake for 45 minutes.
- Remove the foil and continue baking for an additional 10-15 minutes, or until the embutido is firm and cooked through.
- Once cooked, remove the embutido from the oven and let it cool for a few minutes before slicing.
- Serve the embutido slices with steamed rice, pasta, or as a sandwich filling.

# Tapa

## INGREDIENTS

- 1 block firm tofu, pressed and drained
- 3 Tbsp. soy sauce
- 1 Tbsp. vinegar (preferably cane or rice vinegar)
- 2 tablespoons brown sugar or coconut sugar
- 1 Tbsp. vegetable oil
- 4 cloves garlic, minced
- 1/2 Tsp. ground black pepper
- Cooking oil, for frying

Vegetarian tapa offers a flavorful and protein-rich alternative to the traditional beef version. The tofu absorbs the marinade well, resulting in a delicious and satisfying dish that can be enjoyed any time of the day.

- Slice the pressed and drained tofu into thin strips, resembling the shape and size of traditional tapa.
- In a bowl, combine the soy sauce, vinegar, brown sugar or coconut sugar, vegetable oil, minced garlic, and ground black pepper. Stir well to dissolve the sugar and combine the ingredients.
- Place the tofu slices in a shallow dish or resealable plastic bag. Pour the marinade over the tofu, ensuring that each piece is well coated. Marinate for at least 30 minutes to allow the flavors to penetrate the tofu.
- Heat a skillet or frying pan over medium heat and add a small amount of cooking oil to coat the surface.
- Remove the tofu slices from the marinade and shake off any excess liquid. Reserve the marinade for later use.
- Fry the tofu slices in the heated skillet, turning them occasionally, until they are golden brown and slightly crispy on the edges. This should take about 5-7 minutes.
- Once the tofu is cooked, remove it from the skillet and set it aside.
- In the same skillet, pour the reserved marinade and cook it over medium heat until it reduces and thickens slightly, forming a glaze. This should take about 2-3 minutes.
- Return the cooked tofu to the skillet and toss it in the glaze, ensuring that each piece is coated.
- Remove the skillet from the heat and transfer the vegetarian tapa to a serving dish.
- Serve the tapa with garlic fried rice, fried eggs, and your favorite condiments or sides.

Notes

# Longganisa



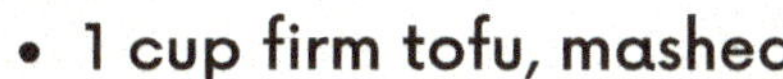

- 1 cup firm tofu, mashed
- 1/2 cup vital wheat gluten or all-purpose flour
- 1/4 cup cornstarch
- 2 tbsp soy sauce
- 2 tbsp coconut sugar or brown sugar
- 1 tsp paprika
- 1 tsp garlic powder
- 1/2 tsp black pepper
- 1/2 tsp salt
- 1 tbsp annatto oil (optional, for color)
- 1 tbsp apple cider vinegar
- 1 tbsp minced garlic
- 1 tbsp vegetable oil (for frying)

A plant-based version of the beloved sweet and garlicky Filipino sausage, made from tofu and seasonings, caramelized to perfection and served with garlic rice and atsara.

- In a bowl, mix mashed tofu, wheat gluten/flour, cornstarch, soy sauce, sugar, paprika, garlic powder, black pepper, salt, annatto oil, vinegar, and minced garlic.
- Form the mixture into small sausage-like shapes.
- Wrap each sausage in banana leaves or parchment paper and steam for 15 minutes.
- Remove the wraps and let them cool before frying.
- Heat vegetable oil in a pan and fry the sausages until golden brown and caramelized.
- Serve hot with garlic rice and atsara (pickled papaya) on the side.

Notes

# Bola-Bola

- 1 cup firm tofu, mashed
- 1/2 cup grated carrots
- 1/4 cup chopped green onions
- 1/4 cup all-purpose flour
- 2 tbsp soy sauce
- 1 tbsp cornstarch
- 1 tsp black pepper
- 1 tsp salt
- 1 tbsp sesame oil
- 1/2 cup breadcrumbs
- Cooking oil for frying

A plant-based version of Filipino meatballs, made from tofu and vegetables, lightly crisped on the outside and served with a sweet-savory dipping sauce.

- In a bowl, mix mashed tofu, grated carrots, green onions, flour, soy sauce, cornstarch, black pepper, salt, sesame oil, and breadcrumbs until well combined.
- Form the mixture into small, round balls.
- Heat oil in a pan and fry the tofu balls until golden brown and crispy.
- Serve hot with a side of sweet-savory sauce and steamed rice.

Notes

# Vege-loaf

- 1 cup milled soybeans (or firm tofu, crumbled)
- 1 cup grated carrots
- 1 cup grated potatoes, squeezed to remove excess moisture
- 1/2 cup breadcrumbs
- 1/4 cup all-purpose flour
- 1 small onion, finely chopped
- 2 cloves garlic, minced
- 2 tbsp soy sauce
- 1 tbsp tomato paste or ketchup
- 1 tsp smoked paprika
- 1/2 tsp ground black pepper
- 1 tsp dried parsley
- 1 tsp dried thyme
- 1/2 cup plant-based milk or water (for binding)
- 2 tbsp cooking oil
- Optional: 1/4 cup chopped nuts or seeds for texture

A delightful and hearty vegetarian loaf made with milled soybeans, grated carrots, and potatoes, flavored with aromatic herbs and spices. Perfect as a main dish or as a savory addition to any meal.

- In a large mixing bowl, combine the milled soybeans, grated carrots, grated potatoes, chopped onion, garlic, and breadcrumbs. Mix well.
- Stir in the soy sauce, tomato paste, smoked paprika, black pepper, parsley, and thyme. Adjust the seasoning to taste.
- Gradually add the plant-based milk or water and the all-purpose flour. Mix until the ingredients form a cohesive, slightly sticky mixture. If the mixture is too wet, add more breadcrumbs; if too dry, add a splash of water.
- Preheat the oven to 375°F (190°C). Grease a loaf pan or line it with parchment paper. Transfer the mixture into the loaf pan and press it down firmly to ensure it holds together.
- Bake in the preheated oven for 35-40 minutes, or until the top is golden brown and firm to the touch. Let it cool for 10-15 minutes before slicing.
- Carefully remove the loaf from the pan, slice, and serve warm. Pair with a side of gravy, mashed potatoes, or steamed vegetables.

## Notes

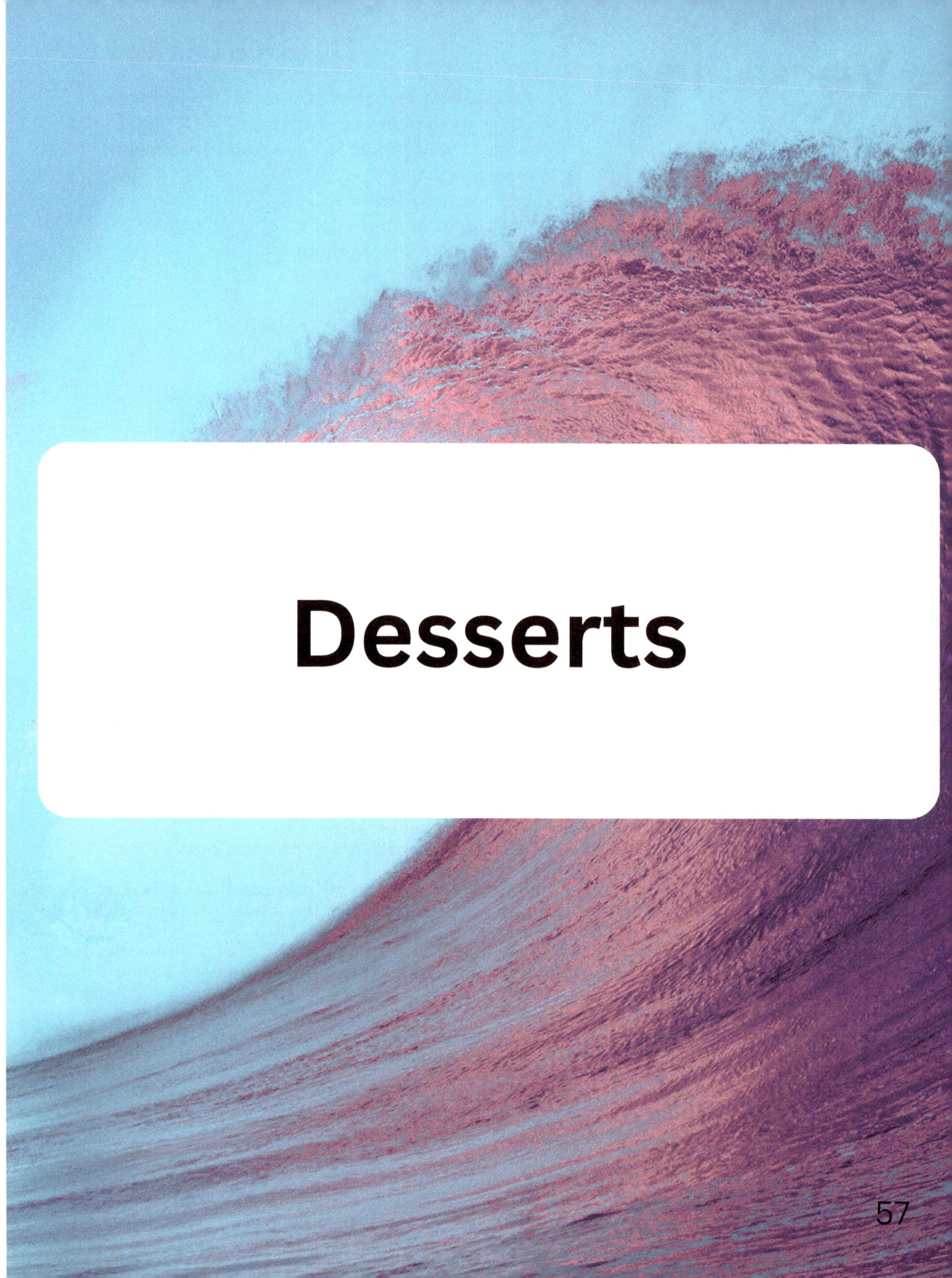
Desserts

# Leeche Flan

## INGREDIENTS

- 10 egg yolks
- 1 can (14 oz) sweetened condensed milk (vegan condensed milk for a vegan version)
- 1 cup coconut milk or almond milk
- 1 Tsp. vanilla extract
- 3/4 cup granulated sugar, for caramel

Leche flan is a luscious and indulgent dessert that is sure to delight your taste buds. Whether enjoyed on its own or as a sweet ending to a Filipino meal, it's a treat that's loved by many.

- Preheat your oven to 350°F (175°C).
- In a mixing bowl, combine the egg yolks, sweetened condensed milk, coconut milk (or almond milk), and vanilla extract. Whisk together until well blended and smooth.
- In a small saucepan, melt the granulated sugar over medium heat, stirring constantly. Cook until the sugar turns into a golden caramel syrup. Be careful not to let it burn.
- Pour the caramel syrup into individual ramekins or a large baking dish, spreading it evenly across the bottom.
- Pour the egg mixture on top of the caramel syrup, gently filling each ramekin or the baking dish.
- Place the ramekins or baking dish in a larger baking pan. Create a water bath by pouring hot water into the larger pan, filling it to about halfway up the sides of the ramekins or baking dish.
- Carefully transfer the pans to the preheated oven and bake for about 45-55 minutes, or until the flan is set. You can check for doneness by inserting a toothpick into the center of one flan—if it comes out clean, the flan is cooked.
- Once cooked, remove the pans from the oven and let the flan cool to room temperature.
- Once cooled, refrigerate the flan for at least 2-3 hours or overnight to chill and set further.
- To serve, run a knife around the edges of the ramekins or baking dish to loosen the flan. Place a serving plate on top of each ramekin or invert the baking dish onto a large serving platter, allowing the caramel sauce to flow over the flan.
- Slice and serve the leche flan chilled. Enjoy!

Notes

# Cassava Cake

- 2 pounds grated cassava (fresh or frozen, thawed)
- 1 can (14 oz) sweetened condensed milk (vegan condensed milk for a vegan version)
- 1 can (13.5 oz) coconut milk
- 3/4 cup granulated sugar
- 3 large eggs
- 1/4 cup melted butter (or coconut oil for a dairy-free version)
- 1 Tsp. vanilla extract
- Grated coconut or shredded cheese (optional, for topping)

Cassava cake is a delightful Filipino dessert that showcases the unique flavor and texture of cassava. Whether you enjoy it as a snack or a sweet ending to a meal, it's sure to be a crowd-pleaser.

- Preheat your oven to 350°F (175°C) and grease a baking dish (approximately 9x13 inches) with butter or cooking spray.
- In a large mixing bowl, combine the grated cassava, sweetened condensed milk, coconut milk, granulated sugar, eggs, melted butter (or coconut oil), and vanilla extract. Stir well until all the ingredients are thoroughly combined.
- Pour the cassava mixture into the greased baking dish, spreading it evenly.
- If desired, sprinkle grated coconut or shredded cheese on top of the cassava mixture as a topping.
- Place the baking dish in the preheated oven and bake for approximately 50-60 minutes, or until the top is golden brown and a toothpick inserted into the center comes out clean.
- Once cooked, remove the cassava cake from the oven and allow it to cool before serving.
- Slice the cassava cake into squares or rectangles, and serve either warm or chilled. It can be enjoyed on its own or paired with a cup of hot tea or coffee.

Notes

# Banana Turon

## INGREDIENTS

- Ingredients:
- 4 ripe saba bananas (or plantains)
- 8 spring roll wrappers (also known as lumpia wrappers)
- 1/2 cup brown sugar
- Cooking oil, for frying

Banana Turon is a delicious and indulgent dessert that combines the natural sweetness of ripe bananas with the crispy texture of the fried spring roll wrappers. You can customize the Banana turon by adding ripe jackfruit filling. It's a delightful treat that can be enjoyed on its own or served with a scoop of ice cream for an extra special touch.

- Peel the bananas and cut them into halves lengthwise. You will have 8 banana halves.
- Lay out a spring roll wrapper on a flat surface. Place a banana half diagonally on one corner of the wrapper.
- Sprinkle about 1 tablespoon of brown sugar over the banana.
- Fold the bottom part of the wrapper over the banana, then fold the sides inward. Roll the banana tightly until it is fully wrapped in the spring roll wrapper. Moisten the edges with a bit of water to seal the wrapper.
- Repeat the process for the remaining bananas and wrappers until you have made 8 turon rolls.
- Heat cooking oil in a deep pan or pot over medium heat.
- Once the oil is hot, carefully place the turon rolls into the pan, seam side down. Fry them until they turn golden brown and crispy, turning them occasionally for even frying. This should take about 3-4 minutes.
- Remove the fried turon rolls from the oil and place them on a plate lined with paper towels to absorb excess oil.
- Let the turon rolls cool for a few minutes before serving to avoid burning your mouth.
- Serve the Banana Turon while still warm and crispy. You can enjoy them as is or drizzle them with caramel sauce or sprinkle them with sugar for added sweetness.

## Notes

# Mango Float

## INGREDIENTS

- 3-4 ripe mangoes, peeled and sliced
- 2 cups heavy cream, chilled
- 1 can (14 oz.) sweetened condensed milk
- 1 Tsp. vanilla extract
- Graham crackers (approximately 20 sheets)
- 1/4 cup crushed graham crackers (for garnish)

Mango Float is a refreshing and delightful dessert that highlights the natural sweetness of mangoes. It's a crowd-pleaser and a perfect treat for hot summer days or any time you crave a tropical dessert. Enjoy!

- In a mixing bowl, whip the chilled heavy cream using an electric mixer until soft peaks form.
- Gradually add the sweetened condensed milk and vanilla extract to the whipped cream. Continue whipping until the mixture thickens and stiff peaks form. This will be your mango cream mixture.
- In a rectangular or square baking dish, arrange a layer of graham crackers to cover the bottom. You may need to break the crackers to fit them into the dish.
- Spread a layer of the mango cream mixture on top of the graham crackers, making sure to cover the entire surface.
- Add a layer of sliced mangoes on top of the cream mixture.
- Repeat the layers by adding another layer of graham crackers, followed by mango cream mixture, and sliced mangoes. Continue layering until you run out of ingredients or reach your desired thickness.
- Finish the top layer with graham crackers and spread a thin layer of the mango cream mixture over it.
- Garnish the top with crushed graham crackers.
- Cover the baking dish with plastic wrap and refrigerate for at least 4 hours or overnight to allow the graham crackers to soften and the flavors to meld together.
- Once chilled and set, slice and serve the Mango Float cold.

## Notes

# Halo-Halo

## INGREDIENTS

- 1 cup shaved ice
- 2 tbsp sweetened beans (red or mung beans)
- 2 tbsp sweetened jackfruit
- 2 tbsp nata de coco
- 2 tbsp sweetened banana or plantain (saba)
- 1 slice leche flan
- 1 scoop ube ice cream
- 1 tbsp toasted pinipig (crispy rice flakes)
- Optional: Evaporated milk to pour on top

A vibrant and colorful Filipino dessert served in a tall glass, layered with shaved ice, sweetened beans, jackfruit, nata de coco, leche flan, and purple yam (ube). Topped with ube ice cream and toasted rice for a festive and refreshing tropical treat.

- Layer the sweetened beans, jackfruit, nata de coco, and saba at the bottom of a tall glass or bowl.
- Add shaved ice on top, pressing gently to fill the glass.
- Drizzle with evaporated milk, if desired.
- Top with leche flan, ube ice cream, and toasted pinipig.
- Serve immediately and mix before eating for a delicious blend of flavors.

## Notes

# Bibingka

## INGREDIENTS

- 1 cup rice flour
- 1/2 cup all-purpose flour
- 1 cup coconut milk
- 1/2 cup sugar
- 1 tsp baking powder
- 2 eggs
- 1/4 cup butter, melted
- Banana leaves for lining
- Toppings: Salted egg slices, grated cheese, shredded coconut

A traditional Filipino rice cake baked to golden perfection, served on a banana leaf. It features a slightly charred top and is topped with slices of salted egg, grated cheese, and shredded coconut for a festive and comforting dessert.

- Preheat the oven to 375°F (190°C). Line a round pan with banana leaves.
- In a bowl, mix rice flour, all-purpose flour, sugar, and baking powder.
- Add eggs, coconut milk, and melted butter. Mix until smooth.
- Pour the batter into the lined pan and bake for 20 minutes.
- Remove from the oven, add toppings (salted egg, cheese), and bake for another 10 minutes until golden.
- Serve warm with shredded coconut on top.

Notes

# Ube Halaya

## INGREDIENTS

- 1 cup grated ube (purple yam), fresh or frozen
- 1 cup coconut milk
- 1/2 cup condensed milk
- 1/4 cup evaporated milk
- 2 tbsp butter
- Optional garnish: Grated coconut, additional butter

A vibrant Filipino dessert made from mashed purple yam cooked in coconut milk and condensed milk. It is smooth, creamy, and garnished with a small dollop of butter and a sprinkle of grated coconut, served in a rustic bowl.

- In a pot over medium heat, melt the butter.
- Add the grated ube and coconut milk. Stir continuously to prevent sticking.
- Pour in the condensed milk and evaporated milk. Mix well and cook until thickened.
- Transfer to a serving dish and let cool.
- Garnish with butter and grated coconut before serving.

Notes

# Buko Pandan Salad

## INGREDIENTS

- 2 cups young coconut strips
- 1 cup pandan-flavored jelly cubes
- 1/2 cup small sago pearls (cooked)
- 1/2 cup condensed milk
- 1 cup all-purpose cream
- Optional garnish: Mint leaves, additional jelly cubes

A vibrant and refreshing Filipino dessert made with young coconut strips, pandan-flavored jelly cubes, and small sago pearls mixed in a creamy base of condensed milk and all-purpose cream. It is garnished with a sprig of mint and extra jelly cubes for a festive and inviting presentation.

- In a large bowl, combine the young coconut strips, pandan jelly cubes, and cooked sago pearls.
- Add condensed milk and all-purpose cream. Mix until evenly coated.
- Chill in the refrigerator for at least 1 hour.
- Serve cold, garnished with mint leaves and extra jelly cubes.

Notes

# Kutsinta

## INGREDIENTS

- 1 cup rice flour
- 1/2 cup all-purpose flour
- 1/2 cup brown sugar
- 1 1/2 cups water
- 1 tsp lye water
- 1/2 tsp annatto powder (for color)
- Freshly grated coconut for topping

A Filipino sticky rice cake dessert with a translucent, orange-brown color, topped with freshly grated coconut. This chewy and glossy treat is served on a rustic wooden plate, making it a perfect afternoon snack.

- In a bowl, mix rice flour, all-purpose flour, brown sugar, and annatto powder.
- Slowly add water while stirring until smooth.
- Mix in lye water and continue stirring.
- Pour the batter into small greased molds.
- Steam for about 30-40 minutes until firm and set.
- Let cool, then remove from molds and top with grated coconut.

Notes

# Puto

## INGREDIENTS

- 1 cup rice flour
- 1/2 cup all-purpose flour
- 1/2 cup sugar
- 1 tbsp baking powder
- 1 cup coconut milk or water
- 1/4 cup evaporated milk
- 1/2 tsp vanilla extract
- Food coloring (optional for variety)
- Small cheese slices for topping

A Filipino steamed rice cake in a variety of pastel colors, including white, yellow, and purple. These soft and fluffy cakes are topped with small pieces of melted cheese and arranged on a rustic wooden plate for a delightful traditional treat.

- In a bowl, mix rice flour, all-purpose flour, sugar, and baking powder.
- Gradually add coconut milk, evaporated milk, and vanilla extract. Stir until smooth.
- If desired, divide batter and add different food colorings.
- Pour into greased puto molds and steam for 10-15 minutes.
- Add cheese slices on top and steam for another 2 minutes.
- Let cool before removing from molds. Serve warm and enjoy!

Notes

# Puto Bumbong

## INGREDIENTS

- 1 cup glutinous rice flour
- 1/2 cup rice flour
- 1/2 cup water
- 1/2 tsp ube extract (for color and flavor)
- 1/2 tsp salt
- Banana leaves (for steaming)
- Toppings:
- Melted butter
- Grated coconut
- Muscovado sugar
- Cheese (optional)

Puto Bumbong is a traditional Filipino delicacy made from steamed purple glutinous rice, cooked in bamboo tubes, and served with butter, grated coconut, and muscovado sugar. It is a festive treat, commonly enjoyed during the Christmas season.

- Prepare the Dough – In a bowl, mix glutinous rice flour, rice flour, water, ube extract, and salt until a slightly crumbly dough forms.
- Shape the Mixture – Form small logs and loosely press them together.
- Steam – Place on banana leaves and steam for 10-15 minutes until cooked through.
- Assemble – Brush with melted butter, sprinkle grated coconut and muscovado sugar.
- Serve Warm – Enjoy with cheese on top if desired.
- Puto Bumbong is best enjoyed fresh and warm!

Notes

# Maja Blanca

## INGREDIENTS

- 2 cups coconut milk
- 1 cup evaporated milk
- 1/2 cup condensed milk
- 1/2 cup cornstarch
- 1/2 cup sugar
- 1/2 cup water
- 1/4 cup toasted coconut flakes (for topping)

A smooth and creamy Filipino coconut milk pudding, presented in square slices on a rustic wooden plate. This slightly firm dessert is topped with golden toasted coconut flakes for a simple yet elegant treat.

- In a pot, combine coconut milk, evaporated milk, condensed milk, and sugar over medium heat. Stir well.
- Dissolve cornstarch in water, then slowly add to the pot while stirring.
- Keep stirring continuously until the mixture thickens to a pudding-like consistency.
- Pour into a greased mold or tray and smooth the top.
- Let cool and set at room temperature or refrigerate for an hour.
- Slice into squares and top with toasted coconut flakes before serving.

## Notes

# Sapin-Sapin

A colorful Filipino layered glutinous rice cake with distinct layers of purple, yellow, and white. This smooth and slightly sticky dessert is topped with golden toasted coconut flakes, making it a festive and inviting treat.

- In a bowl, mix glutinous rice flour, coconut milk, sugar, and condensed milk until smooth.
- Divide the mixture into three portions.
- Add ube extract to one portion, jackfruit extract or yellow coloring to another, and leave the last portion plain.
- Grease a round pan and pour the white mixture first. Steam for 15 minutes.
- Pour the yellow mixture on top and steam for another 15 minutes.
- Lastly, add the purple mixture and steam for 15 more minutes.
- Let cool, slice into neat pieces, and sprinkle with toasted coconut flakes before serving.

Notes

# Binangkal

## INGREDIENTS

- 2 cups all-purpose flour
- 1/2 cup sugar
- 1 tsp baking powder
- 1/2 tsp baking soda
- 1/4 tsp salt
- 1/2 cup evaporated milk
- 1 egg
- 1 tbsp butter, melted
- 1/2 cup sesame seeds
- Cooking oil for frying

A deep-fried Filipino sesame-coated dough ball with a golden-brown, crispy exterior and a soft, slightly dense interior. Generously coated with white sesame seeds, this delightful snack is perfect for any time of the day.

- In a bowl, combine flour, sugar, baking powder, baking soda, and salt.
- Add evaporated milk, egg, and melted butter. Mix until a soft dough forms.
- Shape the dough into small balls and roll them in sesame seeds.
- Heat oil in a pan and deep-fry the dough balls until golden brown.
- Drain excess oil and serve warm.

## Notes

# Suman

- 2 cups glutinous rice
- 1 1/2 cups coconut milk
- 1/2 cup sugar
- 1/2 tsp salt
- Banana leaves for wrapping

A traditional Filipino rice cake made from glutinous rice and coconut milk, wrapped in banana leaves and steamed to perfection. It is served with a side of latik (coconut caramel sauce) and a sprinkle of sugar for an inviting and delicious treat.

- Wash and soak the glutinous rice for at least 1 hour, then drain.
- In a pot, combine coconut milk, sugar, and salt. Stir and bring to a gentle boil.
- Add the soaked rice and cook over low heat, stirring until partially cooked and thickened.
- Cut banana leaves into rectangular sheets and soften them over low heat or by dipping them in hot water.
- Place a portion of the rice mixture on the banana leaf and roll it tightly. Secure the ends by folding them.
- Steam for 45 minutes to an hour until fully cooked.
- Serve warm with latik or sugar on the side.

Notes

# Pan de Coco

## INGREDIENTS

- 2 1/2 cups all-purpose flour
- 1/2 cup warm milk
- 1/4 cup sugar
- 1/4 cup melted butter
- 1 1/2 tsp yeast
- 1/2 tsp salt
- 1 egg

A Filipino sweet bread roll filled with rich, moist coconut filling. The rolls are golden-brown, soft, and slightly glossy on the surface. One roll is sliced open to reveal the delicious sweet coconut inside, making it a perfect snack.

- Prepare the Dough:
- In a bowl, dissolve yeast and sugar in warm milk. Let it sit for 5 minutes until foamy.
- Add melted butter, egg, salt, and flour. Knead until a smooth dough forms.
- Cover and let rise for 1 hour or until doubled in size.
- Prepare the Filling:
- In a pan over medium heat, combine grated coconut, brown sugar, coconut milk, and vanilla.
- Stir and cook until thick. Let cool.
- Assemble & Bake:
- Divide the dough into small balls. Flatten each, place a spoonful of coconut filling in the center, and seal.
- Arrange on a baking tray, brush with milk or egg wash, and let rise for 15 minutes.
- Bake at 350°F (175°C) for 15-20 minutes until golden brown.

Notes

# Taho

## INGREDIENTS

- 1 block silken tofu
- 1/2 cup sago pearls, cooked
- 1/2 cup brown sugar
- 1/4 cup water
- 1/2 tsp vanilla extract

A warm and comforting Filipino street food dessert made with soft silken tofu, arnibal (sweet caramelized syrup), and sago pearls. Served in a traditional clear cup, with layers of syrup and pearls visible, making it a sweet and satisfying snack.

- Prepare the Arnibal (Syrup):
- In a saucepan, combine brown sugar and water.
- Bring to a boil, stirring until the sugar dissolves into a thick syrup.
- Add vanilla extract and mix well. Set aside.
- Cook the Sago Pearls:
- Boil sago pearls in water until they become translucent. Drain and set aside.
- Heat the Tofu:
- Steam or microwave the silken tofu until warm.
- Gently scoop out soft portions to maintain texture.
- Assemble the Taho:
- In a cup, layer warm tofu, arnibal syrup, and sago pearls.
- Serve immediately and mix before enjoying!

Notes

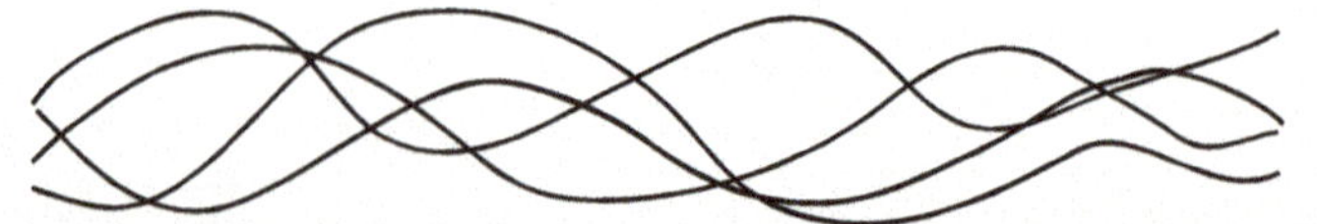

THANK YOU FOR TAKING PART OF D&A³ EXPERIENCE! AS YOU CONTINUE TO ENJOY THIS CULINARY JOURNEY THROUGH FILIPINO-STYLED VEGETARIAN DISHES, WE INVITE YOU TO NOT ONLY SAVOR THE RECIPES WITHIN BUT ALSO TO CREATE YOUR OWN FLAVORFUL CONTRIBUTIONS.

THE BLANK PAGES FOLLOWING THESE RECIPES ARE YOUR CANVAS TO SHARE YOUR UNIQUE CULINARY CREATIONS. JUST AS OUR FAMILY'S LOVE FOR FOOD HAS BROUGHT US TOGETHER, WE ENCOURAGE YOU TO INFUSE THESE PAGES WITH YOUR PERSONAL TOUCH, FAMILY TRADITIONS, AND CHERISHED RECIPES. YOUR ADDITIONS WILL ENRICH THE TAPESTRY OF FLAVORS THIS COOKBOOK HOLDS.

MAY THESE EMPTY PAGES BECOME A SPACE FOR YOU TO TELL YOUR OWN STORIES, EXPLORE NEW INGREDIENTS, AND CELEBRATE THE JOY OF COOKING WITH LOVED ONES. YOUR RECIPES WILL NOT ONLY NOURISH YOUR FAMILY BUT ALSO BECOME A PART OF THIS SHARED CULINARY ADVENTURE.

THANK YOU FOR JOINING US IN CELEBRATING FOOD, FAMILY, AND THE LOVE THAT BINDS US ALL.

HAPPY COOKING!

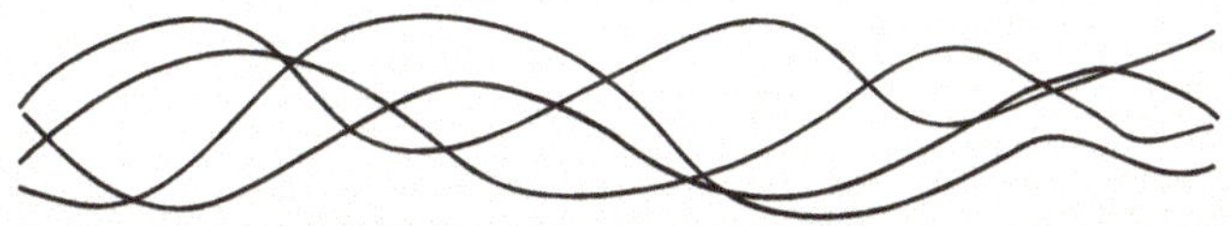

INSTRUCTIONS

## INGREDIENTS

## INSTRUCTIONS

# INGREDIENTS

# INSTRUCTIONS

# INGREDIENTS

# INSTRUCTIONS

## INGREDIENTS

## INSTRUCTIONS

# INGREDIENTS

# INSTRUCTIONS